RECENT PRE-TRIB FINDINGS
IN THE
EARLY CHURCH FATHERS

by

Lee W. Brainard

Soothkeep Press

RECENT PRE-TRIB FINDINGS IN THE EARLY CHURCH FATHERS
by Lee W. Brainard
Copyright © 2023
All rights reserved

Published by Soothkeep Press
(an "operates as" handle for the ministry of Lee W. Brainard)

ISBN — 979-8-9873081-1-0

Cover design by Jeffrey Mardis

The Bible version used in this work is the KJV modified with my own emendations in word order, modernization, and diction.

TABLE OF CONTENTS

PREFACE 5
INTRODUCTION 7
EPHRAIM THE SYRIAN 9
  Introductory Observations 9
  Ten Recently Discovered Pretrib Rapture Passages 10
  Sermon on the Advent, End, and Antichrist 21
  Introduction to Ephraim's Eschatology 31
  Main Points of Ephraim's Eschatology 32
  Differences with Contemporary Dispensationalism 36
  Doctrinal Clarifications..38
  The Pseudo-Ephraim Issue..42
EUSEBIUS 45
  Introductory Observations 45
  Nine Recently Discovered Pretrib Rapture Passages.....45
  Eusebius' Eschatology 57
IRENAEUS..60
  Introductory Observations 60
  Irenaeus is Ground Zero...60
  Contradiction in Irenaeus? 61
  The Correct Handling of Terminology 62
  Irenaeus' Use of the Word "Church" 63

Irenaeus Teaches Two Churches.................................. 65
God's Return to Israel... 66
Jews in the Tribulation.. 67
A Pretribulation Rapture of the Saints 69
Two Classes of Saints in the Kingdom 72
Irenaeus' Dispensationalism 73
THE DIDACHE 75
Introductory Observations... 75
A Robust Prophetic Passage 75
The First Rapture Argument 76
The Second Rapture Argument..................................... 78
The Third Rapture Argument.. 79
The Didache's Eschatology... 80
The Use of Teleioō for Glorification of Resurrection... 81
CONCLUSION... 85
APPENDIX — EPHRAIM'S GREEK WORKS............ 87
ENDNOTES.. 97

PREFACE

In the spring of 2021, I was engaged in an extensive research project in Koine and Patristic Greek literature (250 BC to AD 500), investigating whether the Greek word *apostasia* was used for physical departure. This project was undertaken with regard to the controversy over whether this word in 2 Thessalonians 2:3 is a reference to apostasy or the departure (rapture) of the church. While going through numerous hits on the word *apostasia* in the writings of Ephraim, I stumbled across a rapture passage that I didn't recognize as a known patristic rapture reference. It was so clear, so powerful, that I could hardly believe what I was reading.

> *Blessed is he who unceasingly remembers the fear of Gehenna and hastens to sincerely repent with tears and groans to repent sincerely in the Lord, for he shall be delivered from the great tribulation. [Fifty-Five Beatitudes, 19]*

This discovery led to an ambitious new project — searching for undiscovered rapture passages in the early fathers. One path providentially led to another. As my research progressed, and the testimonies for a pretribulation rapture piled up, my excitement level went through the roof. I felt like I had stumbled upon a treasure trove. Ultimately, I discovered ten clear pretribulation rapture passages. When I expanded the search, I added discoveries in Eusebius, found promising leads in other fathers, and uncovered some overlooked rapture references in Irenaeus and the Didache.

The firstfruits of this research are presented in this volume. But the project continues with studies in the Greek, the Latin, and the Syriac that are either in progress or planned. Lord willing, and if the rapture tarries, I hope to issue a second volume with further pretribulation rapture passages from the early fathers.

LEE W BRAINARD
HARVEY, NORTH DAKOTA
NOVEMBER 15, 2023

INTRODUCTION

This volume presents recent discoveries of pretribulation rapture passages in the early fathers: ten from Ephraim the Syrian, nine from Eusebius, four from Irenaeus, and a three-fold argument in the Didache. The passages from Ephraim and Eusebius are entirely new discoveries. The work in Irenaeus and the Didache builds on a well-known pretribulation rapture passage in each and presents a broader and stronger argument for a pretribulation rapture.

While these passages do not prove a pretribulation rapture — that is the province of Scripture alone — they establish beyond all shadow of doubt that there was a clear and strong pretribulation rapture testimony in the early church and that this testimony survived deep into the patristic era before the militant efforts of the apostatizing church entirely quashed the biblical truth with the error of replacement theology.

This volume also offers an introductory survey on the eschatology of these fathers, presenting their handling of the rapture, the tribulation, the antichrist, and the second coming, their distinction between the saints of this age and the tribulation saints, their distinction between the church age and the tribulation, and their views on such topics as the two witnesses, the mark of the beast, and the place of the temple of God in the tribulation.

There is a lot of work left to be done in patristic research in the original languages, in the early translation languages, and in the available English translations. May this volume help spur vision and excitement in this field of labor.

EPHRAIM THE SYRIAN

INTRODUCTORY OBSERVATIONS

Ephraim, also spelled Ephraem and Ephrem, was known as Ephraim the Syrian or Ephraim of Nisibis to distinguish him from other Ephraims. He was a prominent Christian author in the fourth century (born in 306, died in 373). He was widely respected by his peers and is the most important and prolific of the Syrian fathers of his time. His works were so popular that many were translated into Greek from his native Syriac while he was yet alive, giving them a wide circulation. Many of these works are still used and revered to this day in the Greek-speaking Orthodox Churches.

Theologically, Ephraim was Eastern or Syrian, monastic, and amillennial. His non-literal eschatology makes his defense of the pretribulation rapture particularly noteworthy. In the face of the juggernaut of replacement theology that was crushing all dissent in the church, he stood fast and maintained a pretribulational testimony.

Sadly, the majority of his Greek works haven't been translated into English.[1] The few that have been can be accessed on websites devoted to Ephraim's ministry or patristic theology in general. A good place to start is Roger Pearse's website.[2]

TEN RECENTLY DISCOVERED PRETRIBULATION RAPTURE PASSAGES

For the identification of Ephraim's works, the numbering of Roger Pearse is employed.[3] The numbers used by TLG (*Thesaurus Linguae Gracecae*) are also included for those who desire to access Ephraim's Greek works in an environment with premium tools for searching and lexical research.[4] For identifying passages within Ephraim's works, Phrantzolas' pagination is used.[5] The English translations are my own.

#1 Ephraim the Syrian, *Sermon on Repentance and Judgment and the Separation of the Soul from the Body*

(239) Behold, the kingdom of heaven is at the doors [ready] to flash forth, but we don't want to hear about these things — not ever. The signs and wonders, which the Lord said had to happen, the famines, the earthquakes, the terrors, and the nations in upheaval. These all seem to us like a dream to be told to others. The report of these things does not disturb us, nor the spectacle itself. **For the elect shall be gathered prior to the tribulation, so they shall not see the confusion and the great tribulation coming upon the unrighteous world.** *The season for harvest has now drawn nigh, and the end of the age holds forth. Angels holding scythes are waiting for the nod. Let us fear, brethren, for it is the eleventh hour of the day.*

(239) Ἰδοὺ ἐπὶ θύραις ἐστὶν ἡ βασιλεία τῶν οὐρανῶν τοῦ ἐκλάμψαι, ἡμεῖς δὲ περὶ τούτου οὐ βουλόμεθα ἀκροάσασθαι πώποτε. Τὰ σημεῖα καὶ τὰ τέρατα, ἃ εἶπεν ὁ Κύριος, γεγόνασιν, λιμοὶ καὶ σεισμοὶ καὶ φόβητρα καὶ ἐθνῶν αἱ κινήσεις· ταῦτα δὲ πάντα δοκεῖ ἡμῖν ὥσπερ ὄναρ διηγήσασθαι πρὸς ἀλλήλους. Οὐ θροεῖ ἡμᾶς ἡ ἀκοὴ αὐτῶν, οὐδὲ αὐτὸ τὸ θέαμα. **Οἱ ἐκλεκτοὶ συνάγονται πρὸ τῆς θλίψεως, τοῦ μὴ ἰδεῖν τὴν σύγχυσιν καὶ τὴν θλῖψιν**

τὴν μεγάλην τὴν ἐρχομένην εἰς τὸν ἄδικον κόσμον. Ὁ ἀμητὸς ἤδη ἤγγικεν εἰς θερισμόν, καὶ τέλος ἔχει ὁ αἰὼν οὗτος. Οἱ Ἄγγελοι τὰ δρέπανα κατέχουσι καὶ τὸ νεῦμα ἐκδέχονται. Φοβηθῶμεν, ἀγαπητοί. Ὥρα ἐστὶν ἑνδεκάτη τῆς ἡμέρας.

Technical information
Latin title: Sermo de paenitentia et iudicio et separatione animae et corporis.
Greek title: Λόγος περὶ μετανοίας καὶ κρίσεως, καὶ περὶ χωρισμοῦ ψυχῆς καὶ σώματος.
Greek text source: K.G. Phrantzolas, Ὁσίου Ἐφραίμ τοῦ Σύρου ἔργα, vol. 4, To Perivoli tis Panagias, 1992: 234-244. Retrieved from *Thesaurus Linguae Graecae* (stephanus.tlg.uci.edu).
Work identification: Roger Pearse #60, TLG #61.
English translation source: Translation is my own.

Observations
Ephraim clearly states that the church will be "gathered prior to the tribulation." He adds that the purpose of this gathering is to keep the church from seeing the confusion and the great tribulation that shall come upon the world in the last days. Notice the specific mention of the great tribulation. This is a clear presentation of a pretribulation rapture that has the same spirit as the promise in Revelation 3:10, "I will keep you from the hour of trial that shall come upon the whole world."

The term *confusion* (think *chaos*) is a relatively common term for the tribulation in patristic eschatology.

#2 Ephraim the Syrian, *On the Fathers Who Have Completed Their Course*

(14) Behold, now the holy and the just are chosen and **gathered into the harbor of life that they should not see the tribulation** *and the snares (stumbling blocks) coming upon us because of our sins. ... If we don't now hasten and weep shamelessly, rightly repenting in humility of soul and*

complete meekness, oh how we shall mourn in the tribulation ... Again, when **we see the saints in glory flying off in light in the clouds of the air to meet Christ, the king of glory, but see ourselves in the great tribulation**, *who shall be able to bear that shame and terrible reproach?*

(14) Ὅσιοι καὶ δίκαιοι ἰδοὺ νῦν ἐκλέγονται καὶ **ἐπισυνάγονται εἰς λιμένα τῆς ζωῆς, ἵνα μὴ θεωρῶσι τὴν θλῖψιν** καὶ σκάνδαλα ἐπερχόμενα ἡμῖν δι' ἡμῶν ἁμαρτίας. ... Ἂν μὴ νῦν σπουδάσωμεν καὶ κλαύσωμεν ἀναιδῶς, μετανοοῦντες καλῶς ἐν ταπεινώσει ψυχῆς καὶ πραότητι πολλῇ, πῶς μέλλομεν ἕκαστος θρηνῆσαι ἐν τῇ θλίψει ... Ὅταν πάλιν **ἴδωμεν τοὺς ἁγίους ἐν δόξῃ ἱπταμένους ἐν φωτὶ ἐν νεφέλαις ἀέρων εἰς ἀπάντησιν Χριστοῦ τοῦ βασιλέως τῆς δόξης, ἑαυτοὺς δὲ βλέποντες ἐν τῇ μεγάλῃ θλίψει**, τίς ἄρα ὑπενέγκῃ τὴν αἰσχύνην ἐκείνην καὶ δεινὸν ὀνειδισμόν.

Technical information
Latin title: Sermo in patres defunctos.
Greek title: Λόγος εἰς πατέρας τελειωθέντας.
Greek text source: K.G. Phrantzolas, Ὁσίου Ἐφραὶμ τοῦ Σύρου ἔργα, vol. 2, To Perivoli tis Panagias, 1989: 252-266. Retrieved from *Thesaurus Linguae Graecae* (stephanus.tlg.uci.edu).
Work identification: Roger Pearse #16, TLG #15.
English translation source: Translation is my own.

Observations
Ephraim states that the church shall be "gathered into the harbor of life so that they should not see the tribulation" that is coming upon the world. He also contrasts real Christians flying off to meet Christ in the clouds with false Christians being left behind to go through the great tribulation. The pretribulation rapture cannot be stated in clearer language than this.

Don't be misled by his remark about seeing himself in the time of tribulation. This is not evidence that he believed that the church would go through the tribulation. This is evidence of two things. One, he believed that false Christians would go through the tribulation. Two, he was influenced by the affected humility that characterized the ascetics and monastics in the early church.

#3 Ephraim the Syrian, *On the Second Coming of Our Lord Jesus Christ*

*(407-408) Indeed, the grace of God strengthens and rejoices the hearts of the righteous; and **they shall be seized up in the clouds to meet him. While those who are lazy and timid like me shall remain on the earth, trembling.** ... (409) For behold the Bridegroom is ready to proceed on the clouds of heaven with the glory of his blessed Father. And he will summon each of you by name, and he will place you in the rank of those saints abiding in the unspeakable light in the life that is undefiled, immortal, and eternal, according to your labors.*

(407-408) ἀλλ' ἡ χάρις τοῦ Θεοῦ ἐνισχύει καὶ χαροποιεῖ τὰς καρδίας τῶν δικαίων· καὶ **ἁρπάζονται ἐν νεφέλαις εἰς ἀπάντησιν αὐτοῦ. Οἱ δὲ ὁμοιωθέντες ἐμοὶ ῥᾴθυμοι καὶ ὀκνηροί, τρέμοντες μένουσιν ἐπὶ τῆς γῆς.** ... (409) Ἰδοὺ γὰρ ὁ Νυμφίος ἕτοιμός ἐστι τοῦ προελθεῖν ἐν νεφέλαις τοῦ οὐρανοῦ μετὰ δόξης τοῦ εὐλογημένου αὐτοῦ Πατρός, καὶ κατ' ὄνομα ἕκαστον ὑμῶν φωνήσει, καὶ ἀνακλινεῖ αὐτὸν ἐν τῷ τάγματι τῶν ἁγίων ἐκείνων τῶν διαγόντων ἐν τῷ φωτὶ ἐκείνῳ τῷ ἀνεκλαλήτῳ, ἐν τῇ ζωῇ τῇ ἀκηράτῳ καὶ ἀθανάτῳ καὶ αἰωνίᾳ, κατὰ τοὺς καμάτους αὐτοῦ.

Technical information
Latin title: In secundum adventum domini nostri Jesu Christi.
Greek title: Εἰς τὴν δευτέραν παρουσίαν τοῦ Κυρίου ἡμῶν Ἰησοῦ Χριστοῦ.
Greek text source: K.G. Phrantzolas, Ὁσίου Ἐφραίμ τοῦ Σύρου ἔργα, vol. 3, To Perivoli tis Panagias, 1990: 404-415. Retrieved from *Thesaurus Linguae Graecae* (stephanus.tlg.uci.edu).
Work identification: Roger Pearse #49, TLG # 48.
English translation source: Translation is my own.

Observations

Ephraim once again contrasts those who are seized up (raptured up) to the clouds to meet the Lord and those who are left behind on earth trembling. Notice also the use of *apantesis* (meeting), the same term used in 1 Thessalonians 4:17.

#4 Ephraim the Syrian, *Sermon on the Advent of the Lord, and the End of the Age, and the Coming of the Antichrist*

> Watch always, praying continually, that you may be worthy to escape the tribulation and stand before God ... (116) for if anyone has tears and compunction, let him pray the Lord **that he might be delivered from the tribulation which is about to come upon the earth, that he might not see it at all, nor the beast himself, not even hear of its terrors.** For there shall be famines, earthquakes, and diverse pestilences upon the earth. ... We need to use many prayers and tears, oh beloved, that each and every one of us might be found steadfast in [our] trials, for many fantastic (deceptive?) signs by [the hand of] the beast are going to happen ... (117) ... Finally, brethren, there is a terrible struggle for all those men who are lovers of Christ, (118) **that we may not manifest timidity till the hour of [our] death, neither stand in weakness (sponginess) when the dragon is marking with his own seal in opposition to the cross of the Saviour.** ... (122) And there is nowhere to flee or hide. Everything is in disarray in the sea and on land. This is why the Lord said to us, watch and pray continuously that you might **escape the tribulation**.
>
> (115) ἀγρυπνεῖτε πάντοτε, δεόμενοι συνεχῶς, ἵνα γένησθε ἄξιοι ἐκφυγεῖν τῆς θλίψεως καὶ σταθῆναι ἔμπροσθεν τοῦ Θεοῦ ... (116) Εἴ τις ἔχει δάκρυα καὶ κατάνυξιν, δεηθήτω τοῦ Κυρίου, **ἵνα ῥυσθῶμεν ἐκ θλίψεως τῆς μελλούσης ἔρχεσθαι ἐπὶ τῆς γῆς ἵνα μήτε ἴδῃ παντελῶς μήτε αὐτὸ τὸ θηρίον, μηδὲ πάλιν ἀκούσῃ τὰ φόβητρα αὐτοῦ.**

Ἔσται γὰρ κατὰ τόπους λιμοί, σεισμοὶ καὶ θάνατοι διάφοροι ἐπὶ τῆς γῆς. ... Πολλῶν εὐχῶν καὶ δακρύων χρῄζομεν, ὦ ἀγαπητοί, ἵνα τις ἡμῶν εὑρεθῇ ἑδραῖος ἐν τοῖς πειρασμοῖς. Πολλὰ γάρ εἰσι τὰ φαντάσματα τοῦ θηρίου τὰ γινόμενα ... (117) Λοιπὸν οὖν, ἀδελφοί μου, φρικτὸς ἀγὼν ἅπασι τοῖς φιλοχρίστοις ἀνθρώποις, (118) **ἵνα μέχρις ὥρας τοῦ θανάτου μὴ δειλιάσωσι, μηδὲ στῶσιν ἐν χαυνότητι, ὅταν χαράσσῃ ὁ Δράκων τὴν ἑαυτοῦ σφραγῖδα ἀντὶ τοῦ σταυροῦ τοῦ Σωτῆρος.** ... (122) Καὶ οὐκ ἔστι ποῦ φυγεῖν ἢ κρυβῆναι·τετάρακται γὰρ τὰ σύμπαντα, ἡ θάλασσα καὶ ἡ ξηρά. Διὰ τοῦτο ἔφη ἡμῖν ὁ Κύριος γρηγορεῖτε, δεόμενοι ἀδιαλείπτως **ἐκφυγεῖν ἐκ θλίψεως**.

Technical information
Latin title: Sermo in adventum domini, et de consummatione saeculi, et in adventum antichristi.
Greek title: Λόγος εἰς τὴν παρουσίαν τοῦ Κυρίου, καὶ περὶ συντελείας τοῦ κόσμου, καὶ εἰς τὴν παρουσίαν τοῦ Ἀντιχρίστου.
Greek text source: K.G. Phrantzolas, Ὁσίου Ἐφραίμ τοῦ Σύρου ἔργα, vol. 4, To Perivoli tis Panagias, 1992: 111-128. Retrieved from *Thesaurus Linguae Graecae* (stephanus.tlg.uci.edu).
Work identification: Roger Pearse #53, TLG # 52.
English translation source: Translation is my own.
Abbreviated title: for ease of reference this work will hereafter be referred to as *Sermon on the Advent, End, and Antichrist*.

Observations
Ephraim clearly states that believers will be delivered from the tribulation that is coming upon the earth. This is enforced with the emphatic clarification that they won't see the tribulation or the beast at all. They won't even hear about the horrors of that time.

The warning in section (118) is not a wakeup call that the church will face the dragon and his mark (*dragon* is a patristic term for the antichrist). He has already stated that true believers will not face the tribulation. The warning is a wakeup call for those who merely profess Christianity. Empty professions that manifest fear and apostasy now will manifest fear and apostasy in the tribulation too. Men shouldn't flatter themselves that they will be able to get things together after the tribulation hits. They need to examine themselves now and make sure that they are called and elect. Otherwise, they will face an unpleasant surprise if the end times come in our lifetime.

#5 Ephraim the Syrian, *On Patience and the Consummation of this Age, and on the Second Coming*

> Therefore beloved, faithful servants and elect soldier monks, let us take up in our hearts the full armor which we have been talking about, and without delay meditate on them one by one, that we may be able to fight the good fight and tread down all the power of the enemy, **that we might be delivered from the wrath coming upon the sons of disobedience** and that we might find mercy and grace in the day of judgment before the righteous judge who renders to every man according to his works.

> Οὐκοῦν, ἀγαπητοί, πιστοὶ δοῦλοι καὶ ἐκλεκτοὶ στρατιῶται μοναχοί, ἀναλάβωμεν τὴν πανοπλίαν τῶν προειρημένων ἐν τῇ καρδίᾳ ἡμῶν, καθ' ἑκάστην ἀνυπερθέτως μνείαν αὐτῶν ποιούμενοι, ὅπως δυνηθῶμεν ἀγωνίσασθαι τὸν καλὸν ἀγῶνα καὶ καταπατῆσαι πᾶσαν τὴν δύναμιν τοῦ Ἐχθροῦ, **ἵνα ῥυσθῶμεν ἀπὸ τῆς ὀργῆς τῆς ἐπερχομένης ἐπὶ τοὺς υἱοὺς τῆς ἀπειθείας** καὶ ἵνα εὕρωμεν ἔλεος καὶ χάριν ἐν τῇ ἡμέρᾳ τῆς κρίσεως ἐνώπιον τοῦ δικαίου Κριτοῦ τοῦ ἀποδιδόντος ἑκάστῳ κατὰ τὰ ἔργα αὐτοῦ.

Technical information

Latin title: De patientia et consummatione huius saeculi, ac de secundo aduentu; necnon de meditatione diuinarum scripturarum; et quae quantaque sit quietis silentiique utilitas.

Greek title: Περὶ ὑπομονῆς καὶ συντελείας καὶ τῆς δευτέρας παρουσίας. Καὶ περὶ μελέτης τῶν θείων Γραφῶν. Καὶ τί τὸ τῆς ἡσυχίας ὠφέλιμον.

Greek text source: K.G. Phrantzolas, Ὁσίου Ἐφραίμ τοῦ Σύρου ἔργα, vol. 4, To Perivoli tis Panagias, 1992: 155-179. Retrieved from *Thesaurus Linguae Graecae* (stephanus.tlg.uci.edu).
Work identification: Roger Pearse #55, TLG # 54.
English translation source: Translation is my own.

Observations
Like modern pretribulationists, Ephraim employs phrases like "the wrath coming upon the sons of disobedience" as references to the time of tribulation at the end of the age. The language here clearly has the church delivered *from*, not delivered *through* that awful hour.

#6 Ephraim the Syrian, *Fifty-Five Beatitudes*, 19

*Blessed is he who unceasingly remembers the fear of Gehenna and hastens to sincerely repent with tears and groans in the Lord, for he shall be **delivered from the great tribulation.***

Μακάριος ὃς μέμνηται διηνεκῶς τοῦ φόβου τῆς γεέννης καὶ σπεύδει ἐν δάκρυσι καὶ στεναγμοῖς εἰλικρινῶς μετανοεῖν ἐν Κυρίῳ ὅτι **ῥυσθήσεται ἐκ τῆς θλίψεως τῆς μεγάλης.**

Technical information
Latin title: Beautitudines, capita quinquaginta quinque.
Greek title: Μακαρισμοί, κεφάλαια νε´
Greek text source: K.G. Phrantzolas, Ὁσίου Ἐφραίμ τοῦ Σύρου ἔργα, vol. 2, To Perivoli tis Panagias, 1989: 252-266. Retrieved from *Thesaurus Linguae Graecae* (stephanus.tlg.uci.edu).
Work identification: Roger Pearse #30, TLG # 29.
English translation source: Translation is my own.

Observations
Ephraim's statement, "delivered from the great tribulation," indisputably presents a pretribulation rapture. Indeed, how could deliverance from the great tribulation be stated any more clearly?

#7 Ephraim the Syrian, *Sermon on the Resurrection of the Dead*

(272-273) Give to us a desire, Lord, to watch for your meeting, having the loins of our understanding girded and the intellectual lamp of our soul unquenchable, waiting for you, our God and Saviour Jesus Christ. **Count us worthy, Lord, of the rapture of the righteous, when they meet you the Master in the clouds, that we might not be tried by the bitter and inexorable judgment** *... The righteousness flight is swift, lifting the righteous from earth to heaven. May your grace, Lord, be our strength, and may you take us up in the clouds, with the righteous and the elect in the air, to meet you the king of everything.*

(272-273) Δὸς ἡμῖν, Κύριε, προθυμίαν ἐγρηγορέναι εἰς τὴν σὴν ἀπαντήν, ἔχοντας τὰς ὀσφύας τῆς διανοίας περιεζωσμένας, καὶ τοὺς νοεροὺς λύχνους τῆς ψυχῆς ἀσβέστους, σὲ προσδοκῶντας τὸν Θεὸν ἡμῶν καὶ Σωτῆρα Ἰησοῦν Χριστόν. **Ἀξίωσον ἡμᾶς, Κύριε, τῆς ἁρπαγῆς τῶν δικαίων, ὅτε ἐν νεφέλαις ὑπαντῶσί σοι τῷ Δεσπότῃ, ἵνα μὴ πειρασθῶμεν ἐκείνης τῆς πικρᾶς καὶ ἀπαραιτήτου κρίσεως.** ... Ἡ δικαιοσύνη πτέρα ἐστὶν ὀξυτάτη κουφίζουσα τοὺς δικαίους ἀπὸ γῆς εἰς οὐρανόν. Ἡ χάρις σου, Κύριε, ἰσχὺς ἡμῖν γενηθήτω καὶ ἀναλάβῃ ἐν νεφέλαις, σὺν δικαίοις καὶ ἐκλεκτοῖς εἰς ἀέρα, εἰς ἀπάντησίν σοι τῷ Βασιλεῖ τῶν ἁπάντων.

Technical information
Latin title: De resurrectione mortuorum sermo.
Greek title: Περὶ ἀναστάσεως νεκρῶν λόγος.
Greek text source: K.G. Phrantzolas, Ὁσίου Ἐφραὶμ τοῦ Σύρου ἔργα, vol. 4, To Perivoli tis Panagias, 1992: 256-274. Retrieved from *Thesaurus Linguae Graecae* (stephanus.tlg.uci.edu).
Work identification: Roger Pearse #62, TLG #63.
English translation source: Translation is my own.

Observations

Here Ephraim has the church being caught up to the clouds so they won't "be tried by the bitter and inexorable judgment." He sees the church going up, not through. His reference to being tried (πειρασθῶμεν) by the bitter, inexorable judgment is an allusion to the hour of trial (τῆς ὥρας τοῦ πειρασμοῦ) in Revelation 3:10. He obviously regards the hour of trial as equivalent to the time of divine judgment.

#8 Ephraim the Syrian, *The Destruction of Pride*

*(94) Let us pray the Lord in great humility **that he would take us out (remove us) from the coming fear, and count us worthy of that snatching away (rapture) when the righteous are snatched up (raptured up) in the clouds to the air to meet the king of glory**, and we shall inherit the kingdom of heaven with meekness and humility.*

(94) Δεηθῶμεν οὖν τοῦ Κυρίου ἐν ταπεινοφροσύνῃ πολλῇ, **ὅπως ἐξέληται ἡμᾶς ἐκ τοῦ φόβου τοῦ μέλλοντος, καὶ ἀξιώσῃ ἡμᾶς τῆς ἁρπαγῆς ἐκείνης, ὅτε οἱ δίκαιοι ἁρπάζονται ἐν νεφέλαις εἰς ἀέρα εἰς ἀπάντησιν τοῦ Βασιλέως τῆς δόξης**, καὶ κληρονομήσωμεν μετὰ πραέων καὶ ταπεινῶν τὴν βασιλείαν τῶν οὐρανῶν.

Technical information

Latin title: Ad eversionem superbiae.
Greek title: Πρὸς καθαίρεσιν ὑπερηφανίας.
Greek text source: K.G. Phrantzolas, Ὁσίου Ἐφραίμ τοῦ Σύρου ἔργα, vol. 1, To Perivoli tis Panagias, 1995: 84-95. Retrieved from *Thesaurus Linguae Graecae* (stephanus.tlg.uci.edu).
Work identification: Roger Pearse #3, TLG #3.
English translation source: Translation is my own.

Observations

Ephraim refers to the tribulation as "the coming fear." Fear and terror were relatively common terms for the tribulation in patristic literature. Such expressions ring a little awkward to the English ear, but if we render them as "the coming horrors," the point is driven home to the deepest recesses of our inner man.

Notice that he has the church being removed from earth prior to the time of tribulation to meet the Lord in the clouds. Once again, this is a strong testimony for a pretribulation rapture.

#9 Ephraim the Syrian, *How the Soul Ought to Pray God with Tears*

*(68) Blessed are those who cry day and night that they should be **delivered from the coming wrath**.*

(68) μακάριοι οἱ δακρύοντες ἡμέρας καὶ νυκτός, ἵνα **ῥυσθῶσιν ἀπὸ τῆς μελλούσης ὀργῆς**.

Technical information

Latin title: Quomodo anima cum lacrymis debeat orare deum, quando tentatur ab inimico.

Greek title: Περὶ ψυχῆς ὅταν πειράζηται ὑπὸ τοῦ Ἐχθροῦ πῶς ὀφείλει μετὰ δακρύων τῷ Θεῷ προσεύχεσθαι.

Greek text source: K.G. Phrantzolas, Ὁσίου Ἐφραίμ τοῦ Σύρου ἔργα, vol. 2, To Perivoli tis Panagias, 1989: 59-70. Retrieved from *Thesaurus Linguae Graecae* (stephanus.tlg.uci.edu).

Work identification: Roger Pearse #23, TLG #22.

English translation source: Translation is my own.

Observations

Once again, just like contemporary pretribulationists, Ephraim refers to the tribulation at the end of the age as "the coming wrath."

#10 Ephraim the Syrian, *On the Blessed and the Cursed*

*(323) Blessed are those who cry day and night because they shall be **delivered from the coming wrath**.*

(323) Μακάριοι οἱ δακρύοντες ἡμέρας καὶ νυκτός, ὅτι αὐτοὶ **ῥυσθήσονται ἀπὸ τῆς μελλούσης ὀργῆς**.

Technical information
Latin title: De beatitudinibus atque infelicitatibus.
Greek title: Περὶ μακαρισμῶν καὶ ταλανισμῶν.
Greek text source: K.G. Phrantzolas, Ὁσίου Ἐφραίμ τοῦ Σύρου ἔργα, vol. 3, To Perivoli tis Panagias, 1990: 323-326. Retrieved from *Thesaurus Linguae Graecae* (stephanus.tlg.uci.edu).
Work identification: Roger Pearse #41, TLG #40.
English translation source: Translation is my own.

Observations
As above, Ephraim refers to the tribulation at the end of the age as "the coming wrath." This is identical to the prior citation except that it presents the promise of deliverance in the future indicative "shall be delivered" instead of the aorist subjunctive "should be delivered." This indicates that there was semantic overlap between the aorist subjunctive and the future indicative in both Koine and Patristic Greek.

SERMON ON THE ADVENT, END, AND ANTICHRIST
ENGLISH TRANSLATION

This sermon by Ephraim the Syrian is an overlooked gem that clearly teaches a pretribulation rapture, a three-and-a-half-year-long time of great tribulation, a literal antichrist who administers a literal mark, and the arrival of two witnesses who see souls saved during the tribulation. This is a work that every serious prophecy student should be familiar with.

Technical Information
Latin title: Sermo in adventum domini, et de consummatione saeculi, et in adventum antichristi.
Greek title: Λόγος εἰς τὴν παρουσίαν τοῦ Κυρίου, καὶ περὶ συντελείας τοῦ κόσμου, καὶ εἰς τὴν παρουσίαν τοῦ Ἀντιχρίστου.

Greek text used: K.G. Phrantzolas. Ὁσίου Ἐφραίμ τοῦ Σύρου ἔργα, vol. 4. To Perivoli tis Panagias, 1992: 111-128. Accessed at *Thesaurus Linguae Graecae* (stephanus.tlg.uci.edu).
Work identification: Roger Pearse #53, TLG # 52.
English translation: The translation is my own.

Translation Key
ITALICS — indicate ellipses. Ephraim, indeed the Fathers in general, used ellipses similar to the pattern we see in the New Testament, Koine, and Classical Greek.
PARENTHESES — Indicate alternate translations.
BRACKETS — Indicate material added for clarification.
SMALL CAPS — Highlight references to the tribulation.
BOLD TYPE — Highlight references to the rapture.
NUMBERING — The numbering follows the pagination in Phrantzolas's Ὁσίου Ἐφραίμ τοῦ Σύρου ἔργα, (The Works of Saint Ephraim), vol. 4., a standard work for students of Ephraim.
PARAGRAPHS — The paragraph divisions follow those used by Phrantzolas in his edition of the Greek works of Ephraim.

English Translation
(111) How shall I, Ephraim the least, a sinner full of offenses, be able to speak out on things that are beyond my ability? But seeing that the Saviour in his sweet mercies teaches wisdom to the uneducated and through them enlightens the believers everywhere, and our backward tongues open [the Scriptures] for profit and edification both to me the speaker and to all the hearers. I shall speak with pangs, and I should speak with groans, concerning the end of the present world and concerning the most shameless and terrible dragon, who is about to trouble everything under heaven, and put timidity and contempt and fear in the hearts of men, (112) and perform wonders, signs, and terrors to deceive, if it were possible, even the elect, and beguile everyone with lying signs and deceiving wonders wrought by him. In the allowance of the Holy God, he receives authority to deceive the world because the ungodliness of the world has climaxed, and everywhere every kind of terrible deed is wrought. And because of this, the

incorruptible God assented to try the world with a spirit of deception because of their ungodliness, since men so chose to depart (apostatize) from God and love the evil (the Evil One).

There will be a great battle, brethren, in those times, especially for the believers. When signs and wonders shall be fulfilled by the dragon himself with great authority. Again, when he sets himself forth as if he were God with terrible deceptions, flying in the air, and all his demons lofted in the air before him like angels. For he shall shout with great force, changing their forms and terrifying all of mankind without measure.

At that time, brethren, whoever shall be found walled up [behind spiritual walls] and holding their ground unshaken, having (113) the absolute proof in their soul, the holy coming of the only begotten Son of God, when he sees that UNRELENTING TRIBULATION HAPPENING EVERYWHERE on every soul, completely without relief or rest anywhere, neither on land or sea. When he sees the entire world troubled, and everyone is fleeing to the mountains to hide, some dying from famine, others drooping like a candle from terrible thirst, and there is no one to show them pity. When he sees every face (person) crying and asking with longing, "Is the word of God no longer on the earth?" And he hears, "Not anywhere." Who therefore shall bear those days? Who shall endure the INTOLERABLE TRIBULATION when he sees the commotion of the peoples coming for [to see] the spectacle of the tyrant, and many worshipping before the tyrant, crying with trembling (awe), "Are you our savior?" The sea is tossed, the land is dried, the heavens rain not, the plants are withered, and everyone who lives in the eastern lands shall flee to the west out of fear. And again, those who live in the western lands shall flee to the eastern lands with trembling. When the shameless one assumes authority, he shall send demons into every corner of the earth to boldly preach, "the great king has appeared with glory. Come and see him."

(114) Who has an adamantine soul that he should nobly bear all these snares? Who, therefore, as I said previously, is such a man that all the angels should congratulate him. For I [Ephraim],

mature brethren and Christ-lovers, am terrified by the mention of the dragon, who is preparing for THE COMING TRIBULATION itself, to be among men in those times. What kind of man shall this dragon be found to be? Harsh and relentless in his dealings with mankind. He shall be especially embittered with the saints, who are able to overcome his deceptions. For many shall be found at that time — who are pleasing to God, able to be saved — in the mountains and in the desert places, in much prayer and uncontrollable weeping. The Holy God, seeing them in such inconsolable weeping and sincere faith, shall have mercy upon them as a father's tender compassion, and shall preserve them through that time — they shall be hidden there. For the wholly abominable one shall not cease searching out the saints on land and sea, figuring that he is king over the remnant left on earth and he will subject all of them [to himself]. For the wretch shall figure [that he is able] to withstand [successfully] in that terrible hour when the Lord shall come from heaven, that wretch not knowing his own weakness and arrogance, (115) for which he shall fall. Notwithstanding, he shall roil the earth. He shall terrify the entire globe with lying occultic (magical) signs.

At that time, when the dragon is come, there shall not be rest upon the earth, but rather great tribulation, tumult, and confusion. Deadly pestilences and famines in every corner of the earth. For the Lord himself said with his divine lips, "such things have not happened since the creation of the world." But how shall we sinners liken (portray) its immeasurable, indeed inexpressible, sorrows as God described them? Let everyone set his mind carefully on the holy sayings of the Lord and Saviour. How because of the EXTREME NECESSITY AND TRIBULATION he might shorten the days of the TRIBULATION in his tender mercy, advising us and saying, 'Pray that your flight be not in the winter, neither on the Sabbath. And again, **'Watch always, praying continually, that you may be worthy to escape the tribulation and stand before God.** For the time is near. All of us stand in this evil [of not being diligent], and we do not believe [these exhortations]. Let us pray continuously with tears and prayers, night and (116) day, prostrating ourselves before God that **we** sinners **might be delivered.**

For if anyone has tears and compunction, let him pray the Lord that we might be delivered from THE TRIBULATION WHICH IS ABOUT TO COME UPON THE EARTH **that he might not see it at all, nor the beast himself, not even hear of its terrors.** For there shall be famines, earthquakes, and diverse pestilences upon the earth. The noble soul shall be able to hold his own life together (keep it together) amidst the snares. For if a man be found a little negligent, living recklessly, he shall be besieged, and he shall be taken captive with the signs of the evil and deceitful dragon. And this man shall be found unpardonable in the judgment. For it shall manifestly be discovered that he willingly believed the tyrant.

We need to use many prayers and tears, oh beloved, that each and every one of us might be found steadfast in our trials, for many deceptive signs by [the hand of] the beast are going to happen. For he is God-fighter. He wants to destroy all men. For the tyrant shall work in such a way that all shall bear the mark of the beast when (117) he shall come in his own time with signs to deceive the entire world in the completion of the times (i.e. the end of the age). And this so they can buy foodstuffs and every form of goods. And he shall establish government officials to fulfill the command.

Pay heed, my brethren, to the extreme nature of the beast. The handiwork of evil. For he begins with the belly so that whenever anyone is straitened and lacking food, he is forced to take his seal — not it so happens on any part of the body, but upon the right hand and likewise upon the forehead — the ungodly mark, that he no longer has the right to be sealed [in the spiritual realm] with the sign of the cross in his right hand, moreover completely unable to signify in his forehead the holy name of the Lord or the glorious and honorable cross of our Christ and Saviour. For that wretch knows that the cross of the Lord, if a man be sealed with it, undoes all of his power. Therefore he seals the right hand of man. This is sealing every part of our body. Likewise, the forehead, as a lampstand, bears the lamp of light, the sign of our Saviour on high.

Finally, brethren, there is a terrible struggle for all those men who are lovers of Christ, (118) that we may not manifest timidity till the hour of our death, neither stand in weakness (sponginess) when the dragon is marking with his own seal in opposition to the cross of the Saviour. For he shall work in this manner so that the name of the Lord and Saviour shall absolutely not be named at all in that time. This the weak one does fearing and trembling at the holy power of our Saviour. For unless a man is sealed with his seal, he is unable to be taken prisoner by his deceptions. For the Lord is not distant from such men but enlightens them and draws them to himself.

We need to know, brethren, with complete accuracy, the heartless deceptions of the enemy. For our Lord comes to all of us in the calm, repelling the machinations of the beast for our sakes. We who sincerely bear the steadfast faith of Christ render the power of the tyrant easily rejectable. We procure a fixed and stable reason (mind), and the weak one departs from us, not having anything he can do.

I, [Ephraim] the least, brethren, implore you, Christ-lovers, to not become weak (spongy) but rather strong in the power of the cross. An inevitable struggle (119) is at the doors. We must all take up the shield of faith. Be prepared as the household of faith, not accepting any other course. Seeing that the thief, destroyer, and cruel one, shall first come in his own time, wanting to steal and kill and destroy the elect flock of Christ the true shepherd. For it takes up the character of the true shepherd.

Let us be instructed, O friends, in what form the impudent serpent comes. Seeing that the Saviour, wanting to save mankind, was born of a virgin and in the form of a man trampled the enemy with the holy power of his divinity, the serpent figured to take up the form of his [Christ's] coming and deceive us. — Our Lord in brilliant clouds as terrible lightning shall come upon the earth. The enemy is not coming in this manner. For he is an apostate. — The instrument of that one [the enemy] shall literally be born of a defiled maiden, but he [the enemy] shall not be incarnated. The abominable one shall come in the likeness of a thief to deceive the whole globe. Humble, quiet, claiming to hate unrighteousness, turning back idolatry, honoring godliness, good, friend of the poor, exceptionally handsome, in good standing [good reputation], (120) cheerful toward everyone, honoring the Jewish nation in great degree, for they are expecting his coming [the coming of their messiah]. In the context of all these traits, he shall perform signs, wonders, and terrors with great power. He works deceitfully to please all, so he shall be quickly loved by many. He shall not receive gifts. He shall not speak with anger. He shall not manifest discouragement. With the fashion of a well-ordered man, he shall deceive the world until he shall reign as king.

When, therefore, many peoples and nations shall see such virtues and abilities, they shall all with one mind and with great joy pronounce him king, saying to each other, "Such a good and righteous man has never been found." He shall immediately rebuild his kingdom and slay three great kings in anger. Then he shall be lifted up in his heart, and the dragon shall vomit his own bitterness. He shall trouble the world, and he shall disturb the ends of the earth. He shall crush the whole globe, defiling their souls. No longer as a pious man, but as a harsh, severe, angry, easily provoked, terrible, unstable, fear-inducing, ugly, hateful, abominable, savage, destructive, and impudent man, doing his best (121) to cast all mankind into the pit of ungodliness. He shall multiply signs in great degree, dishonestly and not in truth. Many other nations shall present themselves and praise him through the influence of the delusion. He launches his claim with a powerful voice that shakes the entire place where the crowds have gathered with him, "Understand, all you peoples, my power and authority." He shall move mountains before the eyes of those watching, and he shall raise islands from the sea, all with deception and delusion and not in truth. Indeed, he shall deceive the world and delude the entire globe. Many shall believe and glorify him as a mighty god.

Then every soul shall mourn awfully and groan. Then all shall see UNRELENTING TRIBULATION which besets them night and day, and they find no means to be filled with bread (food). Severe government officials shall be appointed everywhere. And if anyone bears on himself the seal of the tyrant in his forehead or right hand, he can buy a little food from what can be found. Then the infants shall pass away on their mothers' bosoms. Likewise, a mother shall die after her child. Likewise, a father with a wife and children shall die in the market, and there is no one (122) to wrap and bury him. Because of the many bodies tossed into the streets, there shall be a foul smell everywhere which powerfully overwhelms the living. In the morning, all shall count [their remaining family and friends] with grief and groans. When evening comes, they shall count again that they may obtain rest. When evening overtakes them again, they converse amongst themselves with bitter tears, when it suddenly dawns on them, "we must flee the remaining TRIBULATION." And there is nowhere to flee or hide. Everything is in disarray — in the sea and on dry land. **This is why the Lord said to us, watch and pray continuously that you might escape the TRIBULATION.**

Stench in the sea. Stench on the land. Famines. Earthquakes. Confusion at sea. Confusion on land. Terrors at sea. Terrors on land. Much gold and silver and silk garments shall profit no one at all in that tribulation, but all men shall bless the dead, who were buried before the GREAT TRIBULATION came upon the earth. The gold and the silver shall be cast into the streets, and no one will touch it since all abominate it. (123) All make haste to flee and hide, and there is nowhere for them to hide from the tribulation. Indeed, there is more. With the famine and TRIBULATION, there are also terrifying beasts and biting, flesh-eating reptiles shall be found. Inward terror and outward trembling, both at night and in the day. Carcasses in the streets. Stench in the streets. Stench in the houses. Hunger and thirst in the streets. Hunger and thirst in the houses. The sound of weeping in the streets. The sound of weeping in the houses. Chaos in the streets. Chaos in the houses. They shall greet one another with weeping, father and child, son and father, mother and daughter. Men shall pass away in the arms of their friends, and men shall die in the arms of their brothers. The outward beauty of all flesh shall fade. Their appearance shall be like a dead person. Female beauty shall be abominated and hated. All flesh shall fade, as will human desire.

All who had been persuaded [to submit] to the horrible beast and take his seal, the impious mark of defilement, shall run to him together and say with grief, "give us to eat and drink because we are all suffering severe lack in the iron grip of the famine. (124) And drive the poisonous beasts away from us." And the wretch shall answer with great severity, saying, "From whence shall I give you to eat and drink, O men? The heaven is not willing to give the earth rain. On top of that, the earth has not given a harvest or produce at all." The people, hearing these things, shall mourn and cry, having absolutely no reprieve from THE TRIBULATION, but unspeakable TRIBULATION UPON TRIBULATION shall be their lot because they so willingly believed the tyrant. For that wretch is not strong, neither is he able to come to his own aid. How shall he give mercifully to the people? In those days there shall be great distress from the FULL-BLOWN TRIBULATION OF THE DRAGON, from fear, from earthquake, from the roaring of the sea, from famine, from thirst, and from the bites of beasts. All who have taken the mark of the beast and worshiped him, as a good god, they have no part in the kingdom of Christ, but with the dragon who shall be cast into Gehenna.

Blessed is he who is found fully-holy and fully-faithful, who has his heart unwaveringly toward God. Fearlessly he shall resist all his inquisitions, despising both his tortures and his deceptions. (125) But before these things happen, the Lord shall send Elijah the Tishbite and Enoch — how merciful! — that these two might make known godliness to that generation of man and boldly preach the knowledge of God to all, for the sake of not believing the fearful tyrant, crying and saying, it is deception, O men. Let none of you believe him or submit to that God-fighter. Let none of you be afraid. For he shall be destroyed in an instant. The Holy Lord, behold, he is coming from heaven to judge all those who were persuaded by his signs. Nonetheless, there will be a few at that time who chose to hear and believe the preaching of the prophets. The Saviour did this [sent the prophets] that he might demonstrate his inexplicable philanthropy. Because not even in that season does he allow mankind to be without preaching so that all might be without excuse in the judgment.

Then many of the saints, whosoever was found then at the coming of the defilement, pour out their tears like a river in groans unto the Holy God to be delivered from the dragon. And they flee in great haste to the deserts, and they hide in the hills and caves with fear, and they pour earth and ashes (126) upon their heads, praying night and day in great humility. And this [deliverance] shall be given to them from the Holy God, grace shall guide them to appointed places, and hidden in the holes and caves they shall be saved, not seeing the signs and terrors of the antichrist. To those having knowledge, the arrival of this [deliverance] shall be known, but to those having a mind for the matters of life and desiring earthly things, this shall not be clear. For he that is ever enslaved in the matters of life, if he should hear, he disbelieves and abominates the message. Therefore the saints shall be strengthened because day and night they renounce the cares of life.

Then the whole earth and sea mourn. And the air mourns with them, as well the wild beasts with the birds of the heaven. The mountains and cattle and the trees of the plain mourn. And the lights in the heaven mourn on account of this generation of man because all have turned away from the Holy God and believed in the deception, receiving the mark of defilement and God-fighting instead of the life-giving cross of the Saviour. The earth and the sea mourn because the sound of singing (psalming) and prayer suddenly ceased (127) from the mouth of man. All the churches of Christ mourn a great mourn because consecration and offering are no longer conducted.

Now after THE THREE AND A HALF YEARS (SEASONS) of the power and practice of pollution are fulfilled, and when all the scandals over the entire earth have been fulfilled, as the Lord says, next our holy, undefiled, terrible, and glorious God shall come as lightning flashing from heaven, with incomparable glory, with ranks of angels running before his glory, archangels, all being flames of fire, and a river full of fire, with a terrible rushing noise.

Cherubim with their eyes down and Seraphim flying and covering their faces and feet with their fiery wings, crying out with shuddering. Rise up, you sleepers! Behold, the bridegroom is coming! The tombs open, and all the tribes rise in the blink of an eye, and they behold the holy beauty of the bridegroom. And ten thousands of ten thousands and thousands of thousands of angles and archangels, countless armies, rejoice with great joy. The saints and the righteous and all who did not receive (128) the defiling and impious seal of the dragon celebrate joyously. And the tyrant, bound by the angels, is brought with all his demons before the judgment seat, and those who received his seal, and all the ungodly and sinners are bound. And the king shall level against them the sentence of eternal judgment in the unquenchable fire. All who did not take the seal of the antichrist, and all who hid in the caves, shall rejoice with the bridegroom in the eternal, heavenly bridal chamber with all of the saints for unending ages of ages. Amen.

INTRODUCTION TO EPHRAIM'S ESCHATOLOGY

The eschatology of Ephraim is an interesting mix of doctrines familiar to contemporary dispensationalists, teachings that reflect the allegorical, amillennial methodology of his day, and handlings that seem awkward by our understanding of Scripture.

In the following pages, attention will be drawn to where his prophetic system agrees with contemporary dispensationalism and where it differs from it. Readers will be surprised to discover how much Ephraim's understanding of the rapture and the tribulation agrees with that of modern dispensationalism. They will likely be impressed, too, by the breadth of his terminology for these two events. That implies a breadth of understanding. Finally, several problematic passages will be examined where his terminology or his treatment of a subject is so unfamiliar to our theological ears that readers may struggle to understand him.

MAIN POINTS OF EPHRAIM'S ESCHATOLOGY

The core distinctives of dispensationalism

Ephraim held the same core distinctives of dispensationalism that we see in modern dispensationalism: a pretribulation rapture, a literal tribulation, a literal antichrist, saints saved by the gospel in the tribulation, and a distinction between the rapture and the second coming. He also presents a familiar handling of such things as the two witnesses, the mark of the beast, and the earthquakes, famines, pestilences, and terrors of the tribulation.

The same order of events as modern dispensationalism

Ephraim presented the same order of events that we see in modern dispensationalism.
1. The removal of the church for the meeting in the clouds.
2. The raptured church continuing on to the glories of heaven.
3. The time of great tribulation, during which time souls are saved through the ministry of Elijah and Enoch.
4. The Lord's coming in glory.

Clear and robust teaching on the tribulation

Ephraim teaches a great tribulation that is three-and-a-half-years long. See *Sermon on the Advent, End, and Antichrist (127)*.

He teaches an understanding of the antichrist, the mark, and the visitations (famines, earthquakes, pestilences, and other terrors) that is very similar to our understanding. See *Sermon on the Advent, End, and Antichrist (122-125)*.

He teaches that the tribulation ends with a mighty outpouring of God's wrath. See *Sermon on the Advent, End, and Antichrist (126-128)*.

He teaches that the church shall be delivered FROM the tribulation. See *On the Fathers Who Have Completed Their Course (14), Fifty-Five Beatitudes (19),* and *Sermon on the Advent, End, and Antichrist (115-122)*.

He teaches that men will be left behind to enter the tribulation. See *On the Fathers Who Have Completed Their Course (14), On*

The Second Coming of Our Lord Jesus Christ (407-408), and *Sermon on the Advent, End, and Antichrist (115-122).*

He teaches that men will be saved in the tribulation through the gospel ministry of Elijah and Enoch. See *Sermon on the Advent, End, and Antichrist (125).*

He teaches that the tribulation saints will be delivered from the dragon by fleeing to hiding places that God has prepared for them. See *Sermon on the Advent, End, and Antichrist (124-126).*

He makes a qualitative distinction between the tribulation and the time that preceded it. See *Sermon on the Advent, End, and Antichrist (125).*[6]

He distinguishes the tribulation saints from the rest of the saints. See *Sermon on the Advent, End, and Antichrist (128).*[7]

Broad array of descriptions for the tribulation

1. **The tribulation** — *On the Fathers Who Have Completed Their Course (14,15), Sermon on the Advent, End, and Antichrist (115,116,122),* and *Sermon on Repentance and Judgment (239).*
2. **The great tribulation** — *On the Fathers Who Have Completed Their Course (14), Fifty-Five Beatitudes (19),* and *Sermon on Repentance and Judgment (239).*
3. **The trial of the world with a spirit of deception** — *Sermon on the Advent, End, and Antichrist (111-112).*
4. **The trial of the world with bitter, inexorable judgment** — *Sermon on the Resurrection of the Dead (272-273).*
5. **The threatening wrath** — *Response to a Brother Concerning Eli the Priest.*
6. **The coming wrath** — *How the Soul Should Pray God with Tears (68)* and *On the Blessed and the Cursed (323).*
7. **The wrath coming upon the sons of disobedience** — *On Patience and the Consummation of this Age* and *Exhortation on Silence and Quiet.*
8. **The coming fear** — *The Destruction of Pride (94)* and *Concerning Those Who Entice You to Licentiousness.* This rings clearer to the English ear if we paraphrase it "the

coming horrors." English only uses *fear* in the sense of the feeling or in phrases like "that is my fear." The Greeks used it widely in the sense of things that inspire fear, saying fear where we would say something along the lines of *fearful thing* or *fearful time*.

9. **The time of judgment** (ἀπόφᾶσις, apophesis) — *In This World You Shall Have Tribulation.*
10. **The foretold evils** — *Hortatory Sermons to the Monks of Egypt* and *In This World You Shall Have Tribulation.*
11. **The commotion or chaos** — *Sermon on Repentance and Judgment and the Separation of the Soul from the Body (239).* This term is also found in the Latin work *On the Last Times, the Antichrist, and the End of the World*, in which work Grant Jeffrey discovered a rapture passage.

Very clear pretribulation rapture teaching

Ephraim teaches that the church will not go through, but be delivered FROM the tribulation. See *On the Fathers Who Have Completed Their Course (14), Fifty-Five Beatitudes (19),* and *Sermon on the Advent, End, and Antichrist (115-122).* This mirrors the teaching of Revelation 3:10 that the church will be "kept from the hour."

He teaches that this deliverance will involve the church meeting the Lord in the clouds and then going to heaven where they will dwell in glorious light. See *On the Fathers Who Have Completed Their Course (14)* and *On The Second Coming of Our Lord Jesus Christ (407-408).*

He teaches that empty professions of Christianity and the rest of the unsaved will be left behind to go through the time of great tribulation. See *On the Fathers Who Have Completed Their Course (14)* and *On The Second Coming of Our Lord Jesus Christ (407-408).*

He mentions the *apantesis* in the clouds (an allusion to 1 Thess. 4:17) many times. See *On the Fathers Who Have Completed Their Course (14), On the Second Coming of our Lord Jesus Christ*

(405-407), Sermon on the Resurrection of the Dead (272-273), and *Sermon on the Second Coming of our Lord Jesus Christ (39-40).*

Two deliverances of the believers — one before and one during the tribulation

Ephraim distinguishes two qualitatively distinct deliverances in his work *Sermon on the Advent, End, and Antichrist.* The first is a deliverance before the tribulation which removes the church from the scene of the trial (115-118). This is presented with language like "escape the tribulation" and "delivered from the tribulation." The clause "that he might not see it at all, nor the beast himself, nor even hear of its terrors" (116) puts a nail in the coffin of any idea that this might be a deliverance from harm while in the time of tribulation.

The second is a deliverance during the tribulation when the believers who were given the truth through the ministry of Elijah and Enoch (125) are preserved from the savagery of the dragon. God will reveal to them hiding places that he has prepared for them (125-126).

The language used for the deliverance prior to the tribulation is "that we might be DELIVERED FROM the tribulation which is about to come upon the earth" (116).[8] The word *from* here is the Greek preposition *ek*, which means *out of.* Whether the nuance is *remove out of* or *keep out of* depends on the verb it is used with, the context, and the nature of the case. The idea here is to be *kept out of* the coming tribulation. It has the same ring as the promise in Revelation 3:10, "KEEP you FROM the hour of trial which shall come upon the whole world." The language of Ephraim, like the language of Revelation 3:10, simply cannot be construed to mean *delivered through* the tribulation.

The deliverance of the tribulation saints during the tribulation stands in stark contrast to the deliverance of the church before the tribulation. While the raptured church is *kept from* that time, the tribulation saints are *preserved in* it. Ephraim writes of their deliverance thusly, "PRESERVE them THROUGH that time" (114).[9] *Preserve through* is the Greek verb *diatēreo*, which is composed of the verb *tēreo* "keep" and the preposition *dia* "through." The context also describes the manner of their keeping. God will provide them hiding places to be preserved from the antichrist. They will be kept from the antichrist while being kept through the tribulation.

DIFFERENCES WITH CONTEMPORARY DISPENSATIONALISM

His handling of the bride of Christ. Ephraim appears to include the tribulation saints with the church saints in the bride of Christ. "All who did not take the seal of the antichrist, and all who hid in the caves, shall rejoice with the bridegroom in the eternal, heavenly bridal chamber with all of the saints for unending ages of ages." See *Sermon on the Advent, End, Antichrist*, 128. This differs from modern dispensationalism which distinguishes the bride of Christ from Israel. Judging from the fact that he often speaks of the New Jerusalem, Ephraim's view on the bride appears to be at least partly based on the inclusion of both the Old Testament patriarchs and the New Testament apostles in that heavenly city.

Now an inclusive view of all the redeemed is not unique to Ephraim. Many fathers and modern dispensationalists believe that ultimately all the redeemed will be saved in Christ by the blessings of the New Covenant, whether the full company of the redeemed is summed up in a theological concept like *the seed of Abraham* or expressed in a generic manner like *all the saints of all the ages*.

What is unique to Ephraim and other fathers with similar views is applying the title *the bride of Christ* to the full body of the redeemed. Some fathers, like Irenaeus, did a similar thing when they applied the title *the church* to all the redeemed. Modern dispensationalism applies these two titles only to the redeemed of the current age.

He was amillennial and held a general resurrection and judgment. Ephraim, being a convinced amillennialist, held to a general resurrection and general judgment at the second coming.

See his remarks in *Fifty-Five Beatitudes* in beatitude 50, *Sermon on the Second Coming of the Lord*, *Sermon on the General Resurrection*, and *Sermon on the Precious, Lifegiving Cross*. According to this view, all the living and dead, saved and lost, will be gathered at one time in one place and be rewarded. This conception of the judgment is a mishmash of the great white throne judgment, the sheep and goats judgment, and the judgment seat of Christ.

Despite being influenced by the allegorical method of the day, Ephraim still maintained a literal methodology when it came to the rapture of the church. What participation he foresaw for the church at this general judgment, beyond the general concept of gathering and reward, is hard to ascertain from his writings. But it is clear from his handling of the rapture that he foresaw the church receiving much, if not most, of her reward when she meets the Lord in the heavenly city after the rapture.

He applies a broader range of end-times events in the Gospels to the rapture than modern dispensationalists. For example, in *On the Second Coming of our Lord Jesus Christ*, he speaks of the thief in the night, the likeness of lightning, the trumpet, and an earth-rending earthquake that will interrupt the world when the true church is taken to the clouds to meet the Lord in the air and the empty professors are left behind to go into the tribulation.[10] While the trumpet and the thief in the night are quintessential to our conception of the rapture, the notion that visible lightning and an earth-rending earthquake will also occur at that time seems jarring to us, at least to most of us. Such manifestations are not typically associated with the rapture.

His exhortations for men to get serious about the Christian walk are tinged with a performance-based understanding of salvation. In many passages throughout his writings, Ephraim warns men to be diligent in prayer, seeking the Lord, living right, and such like things, lest their Christianity be hollow, and they end up facing such threats at the great tribulation, the great white throne, and eternal punishment.

His principle is true. There are true Christians who are on the road to heaven and will be taken up in the rapture. And there are false Christians who are on the broad road and will miss the rapture, despite their religion, profession, or experience. Men do have an obligation to test themselves and make sure that they are among the called and elect.

But his exhortations are undermined by a performance-based (legalistic) conception of what a man must do to ultimately be saved, a shortcoming that was common in some of the fathers and all of the monastic and ascetic circles. Men were burdened with the duty of pietistic faithfulness to keep themselves out of the tribulation and eternal judgment. In modern dispensationalism, we understand, of course, that true Christians are distinguished by evidence of spiritual life, not evidence of spiritual health, much less exceptional devotion. It is the indwelling Holy Spirit imparted to us for faith, and the blood of Christ imputed to us for the same faith, that gives us the right to salvation, not our superior efforts at obedience, faithfulness, and holiness.

DOCTRINAL CLARIFICATIONS

The rapture and eternal punishment together. Ephraim often treats the rapture and eternal punishment in the same passage. For instance, he contrasts the bridal chamber with eternal punishment in *On the Second Coming*. And he contrasts his rapture understanding of "one shall be taken" in Matthew 24 with eternal punishment in *On the Passage: Two Shall be in the Field*. These contrasts do not imply that he regarded the two events as immediately adjacent or that he held a posttribulation rapture, where the saints get eternal blessing and the wicked get eternal damnation on the same day. He is merely contrasting the two destinies the same way modern preachers do — heaven or hell, rapture or judgment. His own twist contrasts the rapture and hell.

The church mourning. Ephraim's reference to the churches of Christ mourning at the beginning of the great tribulation in *Sermon on the Advent, End, and Antichrist, 127* should not be construed as teaching that the church is in the tribulation. Reading a posttribulation interpretation into this remark not only contradicts his earlier teaching, but it does not fit the context of the mourning. Why is the church mourning? Because consecration and offering have stopped on earth, and therefore God is not honored the way he should be. Why did it stop? Because the church has been removed. If she were still on earth and had merely been forced to go underground, consecration and offering would still be ongoing. In fact, it likely would go to a whole new level. But the raptured church in heaven is mourning because there is no more testimony of God on earth, and the world is heading into deep darkness.

Confusing use of the terms *beast* and *dragon*. Phrases like "repelling the machinations of the beast for our sakes" in *Sermon on the Advent, End, and Antichrist, 118* must not be understood as indicating that Ephraim believed that the church would be present during the time of tribulation. In terminology that seems peculiar to our ears, Ephraim calls Satan *the beast*, a description that the Bible applies to the antichrist. Likewise, he calls the antichrist *the dragon* (*ibid. 118*), a description the Bible applies to Satan. There is a rhyme and reason for this. In his theology, the antichrist is portrayed as a beast because he manifests the beastly character of Satan. Likewise, the antichrist can be called a dragon because he is a reflection of Satan, the dragon. This reflects the observation of discerning men that when God's moral creatures rebel against Him and follow in the dark footsteps of the adversary, they depart from the image of God and descend into the irrational depths of animal-likeness.

Devotional exhortations. In Ephraim's writings, we find numerous exhortations to devotion that are followed by warnings about facing the antichrist or the great tribulation. Many regard these as proof that Ephraim believed that the church would be in the tribulation. For example, we find the following problematic passage in *Sermon on the Advent, End, and Antichrist, (117-118)*.

> *Finally, brethren, there is a terrible struggle for all those men who are lovers of Christ, that we may not manifest timidity till the hour of [our] death, neither stand in*

> *weakness (sponginess) when the dragon is marking with his own seal in opposition to the cross of the Saviour.*

At first glance, the language seems to allow the understanding that the believer needs to be strong now because the church will have to face the antichrist in the tribulation. But a thorough investigation of Ephraim's eschatology and his use of devotional exhortation brings us to a different understanding. The gist of these exhortations is that believers must be strong in their present trials so that they will be counted worthy to miss the tribulation. This is obvious in two exhortations that precede the one above.

> *Watch always, praying continually, that you might be worthy to escape the tribulation and stand before God. (115)*

> *If anyone has tears and compunction, let him pray the Lord that he might be delivered from the tribulation which is about to come upon the earth, that he might not see it at all, nor the beast himself, not even hear of its terrors. (116)*

Notice that the purpose of these exhortations is that the believer may escape from the tribulation, not be preserved through it. The second one emphatically states that the believer will not even see the tribulation. This is in keeping with the pretribulation rapture that Ephraim teaches in many of his works. Now if some of these tribulation exhortations present missing the tribulation as the motive for the exhortation, then we can rest assured that missing the tribulation is the motive for all of them. Ephraim cannot be pretribulational in some passages and posttribulational in others.

Armed with this insight, we are in a better place to understand the original passage.

> *Finally, brethren, there is a terrible struggle for all those men who are lovers of Christ, that we may not manifest timidity till the hour of [our] death, neither stand in weakness (sponginess) when the dragon is marking with his own seal in opposition to the cross of the Saviour. (117-118)*

The point being made can be paraphrased as follows, "There is a tremendous spiritual battle going on for all who profess to love Christ. If we continue in the path of weakness [being a nominal Christian rather than a real one], then we are risking two things. One, dying [as a nominal Christian, which won't be pretty]. Two, [missing the rapture as a nominal Christian and] having to face the antichrist and the mark of the beast in our weakness. Get serious now while you still have time."

We find another tribulation exhortation earlier in the same work that manifests the same kind of warning to be strong now so you won't face the tribulation later.

> *We need to use many prayers and tears, oh beloved, that each and every one of us might be found steadfast in [our] trials, for many amazing (deceptive) signs by [the hand of] the beast are going to happen. (116)*

We can paraphrase this exhortation something along the line of, "Be diligent now, dear Christians, so that you will be strong and firm in your present trials [so that you will be counted worthy to escape the coming tribulation] because many amazing signs will be done by the beast. [Those that are merely going through the motions now are going to be overwhelmed by the antichrist's deceptions.]"

I fully endorse the concept of true believers going up in the rapture and false believers going through the tribulation. However, I cannot endorse the spirit of performance-based salvation that we see in Ephraim's writings, one that was common in his day. The difference in whether or not we go up in the rapture does not lie in our performance but simply in whether or not we are born again. If we are indwelled by the Holy Spirit, then we are going up in the rapture. Those who are born again will manifest evidence of life, but the spiritual health they manifest will range all over the map from very weak to very strong.

THE PSEUDO-EPHRAIM ISSUE

Right or wrong, the consensus view in the academic world is that the majority of the extant Ephraim literature was not written by Ephraim himself but by imitators in the following centuries. For this reason, they are assigned the label *Pseudo-Ephraim*.

Those who hate the pretribulation rapture have often exploited this label to malign the authenticity of the rapture passages in the Ephraim literature and disparage those who cite them as gullible fools who are unwittingly using forged or faked evidence. But this manifests, at the very least, a profound ignorance of the subject. Hopefully, it is not intentional skullduggery.

First of all, the value of the Ephraim rapture passages is not hurt by the designation Pseudo-Ephraim. The label *pseudo* does not mean forgery but anonymity. The label by itself makes no comment on the authenticity, historicity, or value of the work. It merely means that scholars are uncertain who the actual author is. Sometimes the label indicates the author traditionally associated with the work. Sometimes it indicates the author whose content and style most closely resembles that of the unidentified work. Now there are some works labeled *pseudo* that actually are forgeries attempting to exploit someone else's name. But even in such cases, the *pseudo* appellation refers to the anonymity of the actual author, not to the status of the document as a forgery.

Secondly, the value of the Ephraim rapture passages is not hurt by the theory that the majority of the Ephraim works were penned by imitators in later centuries. This theory actually strengthens the case for a robust pretribulation testimony in the early church. If these works were penned by numerous authors in the 6th and 7th centuries, then there was a strong pretribulational testimony much deeper into the Church Age than would be the case if the majority of the Ephraim works were genuine Ephraim productions from the 4th century.

Thirdly, the pseudo label has probably been too aggressively employed with regard to the Ephraim literature. The chief complaint that has been lodged against the general integrity of the whole is similarity. There is a large pile of works bearing his name which address the same themes and manifest a significant degree of overlap in their concepts and expressions. This is typically explained as later imitators affecting his doctrine, style, and terminology in their own productions.

But there is an alternative explanation which, in my estimation, better explains what we see in the Ephraim literature. The wealth of similar but unique Ephraim works is not best traced to a multitude of unscrupulous pretenders, but to the fact that many of his works are transcribed sermons, not theological books. By the very nature of the case, there will be broad overlap in content and expression between different sermons on the same topic by a single preacher. I see this all the time in my own ministry and that of my associates.

Were the usual Pseudo-Ephraim methodology applied to C. H. Spurgeon's sermons a thousand years from now, the "experts" would conclude that many of Spurgeon's sermons were Pseudo-Spurgeon forgeries penned by later imitators who copied his style, themes, and expressions, and who borrowed heavily from each other.

Why is it not regarded as possible that the general harmony of the Greek and Latin Ephraim works is positive and not negative? My own preliminary investigations, in the original and in English translations, suggest that these works bear the same ascetic tone, the same devotional warmth, the same fervent evangelical spirit, the same performance-based gospel, the same eschatology, and the same terms and turns of expression. Does this not suggest that they could, by and large, be penned by the same author?

Furthermore, Ephraim's popularity militates against the theory that the majority of his extant works are imitations. His popularity during his life and for centuries afterward was similar to that enjoyed by Spurgeon. Even heavyweights like Gregory of Nyssa and Basil the Great admired his ministry and learning. According to ancient historians, many of his sermons and works, spoken and written in Syriac, were translated into Greek while he was yet alive and were spread widely in the Koine world. Sozomen claims his works were "no less admired when read in Greek than when in Syriac" (Eccl. Hist. 111.16).

It is difficult to imagine a scenario in which the majority of the hundreds of works that he issued would vanish without a trace within three centuries of his death and be replaced by hundreds of forgeries penned by others. As esteemed as he was, there is little doubt that the monasteries and churches would have exercised a diligent watch over the integrity of the Ephraim collection. Even to this day, his homilies are read and excerpts from them are included in the liturgy in Orthodox circles.

I suspect that time will demonstrate that the strong majority of the Pseudo-Ephraim titles are genuine Ephraim. But whether or not my suspicion proves correct, the Ephraim collection, as a whole, testifies to the existence of a strong pretribulation rapture testimony in the Eastern church in the time of the dominance of replacement theology.

EUSEBIUS

INTRODUCTORY OBSERVATIONS

Eusebius was an influential apologist in the fourth century (born around 265, died around 340). He enjoyed broad influence in his day, being a prolific scholar and the bishop of Caesarea by the sea. His best-known work in our day is his *Ecclesiastical History*. He is another example of a church father who embraced the allegorical method and the amillennial view of the kingdom that prevailed in his day, yet still held a pretribulation rapture. This makes his pretribulationism especially remarkable.

The first passage is the first Eusebius rapture reference that I found. Like my first Ephraim discovery, I stumbled across it while researching the word *apostasia* relative to the controversy over its appearance in 2 Thessalonians 2:1-3. Eusebius' heavenly ark illustration of a pretribulation rapture was so clear, stunning, and forceful that I wrote "WOW!" in my research notes.

NINE RECENTLY DISCOVERED PRETRIBULATION RAPTURE PASSAGES

#1 Eusebius, Fragments in Luke, Luke 17:26

Indeed, as all perished then except those gathered with Noah in the ark, so also at his coming, the ungodly in the season of apostasy ... shall perish ... At the time of the deluge, it (judgment) did not come and destroy all the inhabitants of the earth before (until) Noah entered into the ark. Therefore, in the same way, at the consummation of the age, it (this pattern) says (demands) that **the cataclysm of the destruction of the ungodly shall not happen before those men who are found of God at that time are gathered into the ark and saved according to the pattern of Noah ... all the righteous and godly are to be separated from the ungodly and gathered into the heavenly ark of God.** *For IN THIS WAY [comes the time] when not even one righteous man will be found anymore among mankind. And when all the ungodly have been made atheists by the antichrist, and the whole world is overcome by apostasy, the wrath of God shall come upon the ungodly.*

Ἀλλ' ὡς τότε πάντας μὲν ἀπώλεσεν, οὐ μὴν καὶ τοὺς συνηγμένους ἅμα τῷ Νῶε ἐν τῇ κιβωτῷ, οὕτω καὶ ἐπὶ τῆς αὐτοῦ παρουσίας οἱ μὲν ἀσεβεῖς κατὰ τὸν καιρὸν τῆς ἀποστασίας ... ἀπολοῦνται ... ἐπὶ τοῦ κατακλυσμοῦ οὐ πρότερον ἐπῆλθεν οὗτος καὶ πάντας ἀπώλεσε τοὺς κατὰ γῆν οἰκοῦντας, ἢ τὸν Νῶε εἰσελθεῖν εἰς τὴν κιβωτόν. Κατὰ τὰ αὐτὰ τοίνυν καὶ ἐπὶ τῆς συντελείας οὐ πρότερον ἔσεσθαι **τὸν κατακλυσμὸν τῆς ἀπωλείας τῶν ἀσεβῶν φησιν, ἢ συναχθῆναι εἰς τὴν ἐπουράνιον τοῦ Θεοῦ κιβωτὸν, καὶ διασωθῆναι τοὺς τότε εὑρεθησομένους τοῦ Θεοῦ ἀνθρώπους, κατὰ τὸ παράδειγμα τὸ ἐπὶ τοῦ Νῶε ... πάντας τοὺς ἐπὶ γῆς δικαίους καὶ θεοσεβεῖς ἀφορισθῆναι τῶν ἀσεβῶν, καὶ συναχθῆναι εἰς τὴν ἐπουράνιον τοῦ Θεοῦ κιβωτόν**, οὕτω γὰρ μηκέτι μηδενὸς δικαίου ἐν ἀνθρώποις εὑρισκομένου, πάντων δὲ ἀθέων ἀσεβῶν τῶν ὑπὸ τοῦ Ἀντιχρίστου γεγονότων, τῆς τε ἀποστασίας καθ' ὅλης τῆς οἰκουμένης κρατησάσης, ἡ τοῦ Θεοῦ ὀργὴ τοὺς ἀσεβεῖς μετελεύσεται.[11]

Technical information
Latin title: Fragmenta in Lucam.

Greek text source: *Migne, Patrologiae cursus completus* (series Graeca) (MPG) 24, Migne, 1857-1866. Retrieved from *Thesaurus Linguae Graecae* (stephanus.tlg.uci.edu), Migne 24.584-585.

English translation source: Translation is my own.

Observation on the order of events
1. The righteous are gathered into the heavenly ark.
2. Then follows a season of apostasy when not one righteous man is found, during which time the ungodly are made into atheists by the antichrist.
3. Then the wrath of God is poured out upon the ungodly.

Observation — the same events in modern terminology
1. The rapture
2. The tribulation
3. The second coming

Other observations
The antichrist and the apostasy are sandwiched between the rapture and the second coming.

The removal of the church introduces the time of apostasy. Note the explanatory phrase "in this way."

The flood waters piled up on earth over the course of time. In the same way, the judgments at the end of the age will pile up over the course of time.

#2 Eusebius, Fragments in Luke, Luke 18:1-8

There was a judge who did not fear God." ... The saying "When the Son of man comes, shall he find faith on earth" reveals a lapse of faith, when no faithful man shall be found, or perhaps somewhere a few scarce ones in the time of his second theophany. For the world shall meet with a great test in the season of apostasy, in which the faithful man will scarcely be found. **Suddenly, there shall not even be one, because some have been taken, and the others left**

behind, delivered to the eagles. *In this way, there shall be a lapse of faith among mankind, thereafter he shall take revenge for his saints who had been killed by the ungodly.*

«Κριτής τις ἦν τὸν Θεὸν μὴ φοβούμενος.» … τὸ δὲ εἰπεῖν «Ἆρα ἐλθὼν ὁ Υἱὸς τοῦ ἀνθρώπου εὑρήσει τὴν πίστιν ἐπὶ τῆς γῆς;» ἔκλειψιν δηλοῖ τῆς πίστεως, ὡς μηδένα πιστὸν εὑρεθήσεσθαι, ἢ εἴ που ἄρα σπάνιόν τινα κατὰ τὸν τῆς δευτέρας αὐτοῦ θεοφανείας χρόνον. Ὅπερ μέγα τεκμήριον τυγχάνει τοῦ καιροῦ τῆς ἀποστασίας, ἐν ᾧ σπάνιος ἔσται ὁ εὑρεθησόμενος πιστός. **τάχα δὲ οὐδὲ εἷς ἔσται, διὰ τὸ τοὺς μὲν παραληφθήσεσθαι, τοὺς δὲ καταλειφθήσεσθαι τοῖς ἀετοῖς παραδοθησομένους.** οὕτω τε ἐξ ἀνθρώπων ἐκλειπούσης τῆς πίστεως, αὐτὸς λοιπὸν ἐπιστήσεται τὴν ἐκδίκησιν ποιησόμενος τῶν ἁγίων αὐτοῦ τῶν ὑπὸ τῶν ἀσεβῶν ἀνῃρημένων.

Technical information
Latin title: Fragmenta in Lucam
Greek text source: *Migne, Patrologiae cursus completus* (series Graeca) (MPG) 24, Migne, 1857-1866. Retrieved from *Thesaurus Linguae Graecae* (stephanus.tlg.uci.edu), Migne 24.588.
English translation source: Translation is my own.

Observation on the order of events
1. The sudden disappearance of the church — "some taken, others left."
2. The lapse of faith (the season of apostasy) is introduced after the church is taken.
3. God's judgment (vengeance) follows the season of apostasy.

Observation — the same events in modern terminology
1. The rapture
2. The tribulation
3. The second coming.

Other observations
The *season of apostasy* and *the lapse of faith* are synonyms and refer to the same time frame.
The removal of the church introduces the time of apostasy.
Note the explanatory phrase "in this way."
Wrath follows the tribulation. Note the word "thereafter."

#3 Eusebius, Fragments in Daniel, fragment ε

Hence, I think the apostle Paul was moved to write in this manner on the second coming of Christ, "For the Lord himself shall descend from heaven with a command, with the call of the archangel, and with the trumpet of God," and so forth. **But the same apostle also set forth in order FOLLOWING THIS PROPHECY the end-times coming of the antichrist and his depravity and the glorious appearing of our Saviour.**

Ἐντεῦθεν οἶμαι τὸν ἀπόστολον Παῦλον ὁρμᾶσθαι περὶ τῆς δευτέρας ἀφίξεως τοῦ Χριστοῦ γράφοντα τοιάδε, Ὅτι αὐτὸς ὁ Κύριος ἐν κελεύσματι, ἐν φωνῇ ἀρχαγγέλου καὶ ἐν σάλπιγγι Θεοῦ καταβήσεται ἀπ' οὐρανοῦ, καὶ τὰ ἑξῆς. Ὁ δ' αὐτὸς ἀπόστολος καὶ τὴν ὑστάτην τοῦ Ἀντιχρίστου ἄφιξιν τὴν καὶ ἀπώλειαν, καὶ ἐπὶ ταύτῃ τὴν τοῦ Σωτῆρος ἡμῶν ἔνδοξον παρουσίαν ἀκολούθως τῇ προφητείᾳ παρίστησι λέγων.

Technical information
Latin title: Fragmenta in Danielem.
Greek text source: *Migne, Patrologiae cursus completus* (series Graeca) (MPG) 24, Migne, 1857-1866. Retrieved from *Thesaurus Linguae Graecae* (stephanus.tlg.uci.edu), Migne 24.528.
English translation source: Translation is my own.

Observation on the order of events
1. The descent of the Lord to gather the church
2. The coming of the antichrist
3. The glorious public appearing of the Lord

Observation — the same events in modern terminology
1. The rapture
2. The tribulation
3. The second coming.

Observations

Eusebius sandwiched the time of the antichrist between the rapture and the glorious appearance.

The adverb *akolouthōs* means *follow in order* in such contexts (see Lampe), so its use here implies that the antichrist and the glorious appearance of the Lord follow the rapture in order.

The word *apōleia* is used here in the patristic sense of *depravity* (see Lampe).

#4 Eusebius, Commentary in Psalms, Psalm 75

*All over again I shall exalt the horns of the righteous, since they were humbled (humiliated). Then they shall be exalted when they shall reign with their own king according to the apostle who said, "**For the first fruits is Christ, then those who are Christ's in his parousia, then the end, when he shall deliver the kingdom to his God and Father, when he shall destroy all authority and power.**" When the righteous shall drink the cup of life eternal, which very thing he promised them saying, "until I would drink it new with you in the kingdom of heaven."*

Ἀνάπαλιν δὲ τὰ τοῦ δικαίου κέρατα ὑψώσω, ἐπείπερ ἦν τεταπεινωμένα. Τότε δὲ ὑψωθήσεται, ἐπειδὰν συμβασιλεύῃ τῷ ἑαυτοῦ βασιλεῖ κατὰ τὸν Ἀπόστολον, ὅς φησιν «**Ἀπαρχὴ γὰρ Χριστός, εἶτα οἱ τοῦ Χριστοῦ ἐν τῇ παρουσίᾳ αὐτοῦ, εἶτα τὸ τέλος, ὅταν παραδιδῷ τὴν βασιλείαν τῷ Θεῷ καὶ Πατρί, ὅταν καταργήσῃ πᾶσαν ἐξουσίαν καὶ δύναμιν.**» Ὅτε καὶ πίονται οἱ δίκαιοι ποτήριον ζωῆς ἀθανάτου, ὅπερ αὐτοῖς ἐπήγγελται εἰπών, «Ἕως ἂν πίω αὐτὸ καινὸν μεθ' ὑμῶν ἐν τῇ βασιλείᾳ τῶν οὐρανῶν.»

Technical information
Latin title: Commentaria in Psalmos
Greek text source: *Migne, Patrologiae cursus completus* (series Graeca) (MPG) 23, Migne, 1857-1866. Retrieved from *Thesaurus Linguae Graecae* (stephanus.tlg.uci.edu), Migne 23.876.
English translation source: Translation is my own.

Observe the order of events
1. The resurrection of Christ
2. The resurrection of the church at Christ's parousia
3. The end when the kingdom delivered to the Father

Other observations
It must be noted that Eusebius is an amillennialist, so his end when the kingdom is delivered to the Father comes at the second coming of Christ, not after the earthly, thousand-year reign of Christ. This means his distinction between the parousia and the end is the same as modern pretribulationists make between the rapture and the second coming.

#5 Eusebius, Commentary in Psalms, Psalm 42:5

Symmachus states it thusly, "Because I shall come forth unto my tabernacle, I shall bring myself to the house of God, with the sound of praise and confession of the celebrating multitudes." Or, according to Aquila, "with the praise and thanksgiving of the feasting crowd." It presents what is the end (reward) of those who in this present life are genuinely awaiting all that is coming. For the thrice-blessed end shall come upon them, the amazing tabernacle of God, even his house within her, in which the worthy are contained, and **they shall be brought into [his presence], being carried aloft by the angelic host.** *Which even the apostle spoke knowingly of,* **"We shall be caught up in the clouds to meet the Lord in the air, and so we shall ever be with the Lord."**

Λέγων δὲ ὁ Σύμμαχος, «Ὅτι ἐξελεύσομαι εἰς τὴν σκηνὴν, διαβασταχθήσομαι ἕως τοῦ οἴκου τοῦ Θεοῦ, μετὰ φωνῆς εὐφημίας καὶ ἐξομολογήσεως πλήθους πανηγυριζόντων,» ἢ κατὰ τὸν Ἀκύλαν, «Αἰνέσεως καὶ εὐχαριστίας ὄχλου ἑορτάζοντος» παρίστη ὁποῖον ἔσται τὸ τέλος τῶν ἐν τῷ παρόντι βίῳ πᾶν τὸ ἐπιὸν γενναίως ὑπομενόντων. Διαδέξεται γὰρ τούτους τὸ τρισμακάριον τέλος, ἡ θαυμαστὴ σκηνὴ τοῦ Θεοῦ, καὶ ὁ ἐνδοτάτω αὐτῆς οἶκος αὐτοῦ, ἐν ᾧ **οἱ ἄξιοι διαβασταζόμενοι, καὶ μετέωροι ὑπὸ ἀγγελικῶν δυνάμεων αἰρόμενοι εἰσαχθήσονται**. Ἃ δὴ καὶ ὁ Ἀπόστολος εἰδὼς ἔλεγεν «**Ἁρπαγησόμεθα ἐν νεφέλαις εἰς ἀπάντησιν τοῦ Κυρίου εἰς ἀέρα, καὶ οὕτω πάντοτε σὺν Κυρίῳ ἐσόμεθα.**»

Technical information
Latin title: Commentaria in Psalmos
Greek text source: *Migne, Patrologiae cursus completus* (series Graeca) (MPG) 23, Migne, 1857-1866. Retrieved from *Thesaurus Linguae Graecae* (stephanus.tlg.uci.edu), Migne 23.373.
English translation source: Translation is my own.

Observe the main points
1. The Lord comes unto his temple [the church].
2. The church shall be gathered and carried aloft by angels.
3. This is the promise in 1 Thessalonians. 4:13-18.
4. This is the promised reward for all those genuinely waiting for the Lord's coming.

Other observations
We know from other Eusebius passages, such as *Commentary on Isaiah 2.58*, that he believes that the church will be taken to the heavenly city when she meets her Lord in the clouds. So we can rest assured that he had the precious promise of John 14:1-3 in mind in all of his gathering in the clouds passages. The next time the Lord physically interacts with his church, he is taking them to the Father's house in heaven.

We know from other gathering-in-the-air passages in Eusebius that he views this glorious meeting as a pretribulational event.

#6 Eusebius, General Elementary Introduction, Point 31 "On Him"

WHEN *he has finished his spiritual temple of rational and soulish stones, that is his church, the Lord himself shall come, even the* GOD *Word, and with him the angel of the covenant, to the manifested temple.* THEN, *foreannouncing the things of his second coming, the Word says to the sinners, "Behold the Lord Almighty comes, and who shall endure the day of his entrance? Who shall stand in his appearance?"*

Ὅτε ἐκ λογικῶν καὶ ἐμψύχων λίθων τὸν πνευματικὸν ναὸν, τοῦτ' ἔστιν τὴν ἐκκλησίαν, ἐπισκευάσαντος αὐτοῦ, ἥξει αὐτὸς ὁ Κύριος καὶ Θεὸς Λόγος ἅμα αὐτῷ τῷ τῆς διαθήκης ἀγγέλῳ εἰς τὸν δεδηλωμένον ναόν, **εἶτα**, οἷα τὴν δευτέραν αὐτοῦ παρουσίαν προαγγέλλων, ὁ Λόγος ὡς πρὸς τοὺς ἁμαρτωλοὺς φησὶν, «ἰδοὺ ἔρχεται Κύριος παντοκράτωρ, καὶ τίς ὑπομενεῖ ἡμέραν εἰσόδου αὐτοῦ; ἢ τίς ὑποστήσεται ἐν τῇ ὀπτασίᾳ αὐτοῦ;»

Technical information
Latin title: Generalis elementaria introduction
Greek text source: T. Gaisford, *Eusebii Pamphili episcopi Caesariensis eclogae propheticae*, Oxford University Press, 1842. Retrieved from *Thesaurus Linguae Graecae* (stephanus.tlg.uci.edu), Gaisford, pp. 132-333.
English translation source: Translation is my own.

Observe the order of events
1. The Lord shall finish his temple (the church).
2. The Lord shall come to his finished temple.
3. After the Lord comes to his temple, he foreannounces the awful judgment of the 2nd coming.

Observe the *when, then* construction
1. WHEN the spiritual temple is completed, the Lord comes to it, THEN the Lord announces the second coming.
2. IF Eusebius believed that the second coming will be yet future when the Lord comes to his temple (the church), THEN he believed that the rapture and the second coming are distinct events that are separated by time.

#7 Eusebius, Commentary on Isaiah, Book 1, Sect. 54

But "as in Adam we all die," according to the apostle, "so in Christ we shall all be made alive." Since, moreover, **"Christ is the first fruits of the new age, then those who are Christ's at his parousia, then the end."** *On this account he would be called the father of the coming age and again the prince of peace.*

ἀλλ' «ὥσπερ ἐν τῷ Ἀδὰμ πάντες ἀποθνῄσκομεν» κατὰ τὸν Ἀπόστολον, «οὕτως ἐν τῷ Χριστῷ πάντες ζωοποιηθησόμεθα.» ἐπεὶ τοίνυν τοῦ νέου αἰῶνος «**ἀπαρχὴ Χριστός, ἔπειτα οἱ τοῦ Χριστοῦ ἐν τῇ παρουσίᾳ αὐτοῦ, εἶτα τὸ τέλος,**» τούτου χάριν πατὴρ τοῦ μέλλοντος αἰῶνος ἂν εἴρηται καὶ πάλιν εἰρήνης ἄρχων.

Technical information
Latin title — Commentarius in Isaiam
Greek text source — J. Ziegler, *Eusebius Werke, Band 9, Der Jesajakommentar,* Akademie Verlag, 1975. Retrieved from *Thesaurus Linguae Graecae* (stephanus.tlg.uci.edu).
English translation source — Translation is my own.

Observe the order of events
1. Christ is the firstfruits of the new age.
2. Then those who belong to Christ at his *parousia*.
3. Then the *end*.

Observe his use of *parousia* and *end*
Once again it must be noted that Eusebius was amillennial. Therefore, his *end* can only be the second coming, and his *parousia* can only be a preceding rapture of the church.

What Eusebius here terms the *end*, he elsewhere terms the second coming, the coming in glory, the delivery of the kingdom to the Father.

His employment of *parousia* as a technical term for the rapture most likely stems from 1 Thessalonians 4:13-18 and 2 Thessalonians 2:1-3.

#8 Eusebius, Commentary on Isaiah, Book 2, Sect. 24, (Is.43:5-6)

Many sons, born by God, I shall gather into my heavenly city, taking them up, flying them through the air, lofted like birds on the winds — I am talking about angelic powers. Some of them I shall gather to myself from the north, others from Africa, or as others say it, from the south.

πολλὰ τέκνα κατὰ θεὸν γεννήσας συνάξω εἰς τὴν ἐπουράνιόν μου πόλιν μετεώρους αὐτοὺς ἀναλαβὼν δι' ἀέρος ὥσπερ πτηνοῖς ἀνέμοις ὑποκουφιζομένους, λέγω δὲ ἀγγελικαῖς δυνάμεσι. καὶ τοὺς μὲν ἀπὸ βορρᾶ παραλήψομαι, τοὺς δὲ ἀπὸ λιβός, ἢ κατὰ τοὺς λοιποὺς ἑρμηνευτάς, ἀπὸ νότου.

Technical information:
Latin title: Commentarius in Isaiam
Greek text source: J. Ziegler, *Eusebius Werke, Band 9, Der Jesajakommentar*, Akademie Verlag, 1975. Retrieved from *Thesaurus Linguae Graecae* (stephanus.tlg.uci.edu).
English translation source: Translation is my own.

Observe the rich diversity of rapture terms
1. συνάγω *sunagō* "gather" — compare *synagogue*
2. μετέωρος *meteōros* "flying" — compare *meteor*
3. ἀναλαμβάνω *analambanō* "take up"
4. παραλαμβάνω *paralambanō* "gather"
5. ὑποκουφίζω *upokoufidzō* "loft"

Other observations
The born-again sons of God shall be taken up and flown through the air with their ultimate destiny being the heavenly city. This is a rapture passage reminiscent of John 14:1-3.

#9 Eusebius, Commentary on Isaiah, Bk. 2, Sect. 58

In the season of the end, God shall bring them to the city of God, even the heavenly Jerusalem, and prosper them with this supreme boon, when he shall take them up like he did with Elijah, carrying them upon angelic chariots, bathing them in heavenly light ... in regard to the sense, the lofted journey through the air signifies the carrying [of the church] into the heavens, which being interpreted more wisely the divine apostle said, "we shall be seized in the clouds to meet the Lord in the air, and so we shall always be with the Lord." So they shall enter into the heavenly city. So all the Gentiles who have been saved shall come into the heavenly Jerusalem.

κατὰ δὲ τὸν καιρὸν τῆς συντελείας ἐπὶ τὴν τοῦ θεοῦ πόλιν καὶ τὴν ἐπουράνιον Ἰερουσαλὴμ ἄξουσιν αὐτοὺς τέλος ἀγαθὸν αὐτοῖς τοῦτο προχωρήσαντες, ὅτε καὶ ἀναληφθήσονται ὁμοίως τῷ Ἠλίᾳ ἐφ' ἁρμάτων ἀγγελικῶν ὀχούμενοι φωτὸς ἐπουρανίου περιαστράπτοντος αὐτούς ... κατὰ δὲ τὴν διάνοιαν τὴν δι' ἀέρος μετάρσιον αὐτῶν πορείαν τὴν εἰς οὐρανοὺς φέρουσαν σημαίνει, ἣν ἑρμηνεύων ἐπὶ τὸ σαφέστερον ὁ θεῖος Ἀπόστολος ἔλεγεν, «ἁρπαγησόμεθα ἐν νεφέλαις εἰς ἀπάντησιν τοῦ κυρίου εἰς ἀέρα, καὶ οὕτως πάντοτε σὺν κυρίῳ ἐσόμεθα.» οὕτω δὲ εἰσελεύσονται εἰς τὴν ἐπουράνιον τοῦ θεοῦ πόλιν, οὕτω δὲ ἥξουσιν οἱ ἐξ ἁπάντων τῶν ἐθνῶν σῳζόμενοι εἰς τὴν ἐπουράνιον Ἱερουσαλήμ.

Technical information
Latin title: Commentarius in Isaiam
Greek text source: J. Ziegler, *Eusebius Werke, Band 9, Der Jesajakommentar*, Akademie Verlag, 1975. Retrieved from *Thesaurus Linguae Graecae* (stephanus.tlg.uci.edu).
English translation source: Translation is my own.

Observe the rich diversity of rapture expressions
1. "bring them to the city of God"
2. "take them up like he did with Elijah"
3. "lofted journey through the air"
4. "carrying [of the church] into the heavens"
5. "seized in the clouds to meet the Lord in the air"

Other observations
The church shall be lofted through the air and carried to the heavens. This is another rapture passage of the same spirit as John 14:1-3 where the saints are taken to the Father's house.

EUSEBIUS' ESCHATOLOGY

Eusebius taught a pretribulation rapture that is identical to modern pretribulationism in its salient details. He held that the church would first be removed from earth prior to the tribulation, then the tribulation would unfold on earth under the evil headship of the antichrist, and finally, the Lord would descend from heaven in judgment at the second coming.

He employed a variety of terms and descriptions for the tribulation. the season of apostasy, the apostasy, the time of the antichrist and his depravity, and the cataclysm of the destruction of the ungodly. This can be slightly jarring to those influenced by modern dispensationalism which leans heavily on the word *tribulation*. His favored term for this time was the *apostasy*.

His handling of the rapture is presented in biblical themes that are familiar to the modern rapture believer. The raptured believers first meet the Lord in the clouds, then they continue on to the heavenly city. Noah's deliverance prior to the flood is a type of the church's deliverance before the time of the antichrist. Elijah is a type of the rapture. One taken and the other left is applied to one taken in the rapture and the other left behind to go into the tribulation. The rapture of the church is pictured as flying away. The church is regarded as the spiritual temple. The rapture is the Lord coming to his spiritual temple.

He used a rich diversity of terms for the rapture. Many are ones we are familiar with from the Bible: gather (*sunagō*), take up (*analambanō*), sieze (*harpazō*), gather (*paralambanō*), and coming (*parousia*). But he also employed terms that we do not see in the Bible, such as flying (*meteōros*), loft (*hupokouphizō*), and lofted journey (*metarsion poreian*). This varied handling of the rapture implies that we are not mistaken in seeing a rapture in his writings. The more clarifying descriptions you have for a thing, the less likely you are to misidentify and misunderstand it.

He employed a rich diversity of contrasts between the rapture and the second coming. He contrasted the church being gathered into the heavenly ark with the end or consummation (*sunteleia*). He contrasted the "one shall be taken" scenario with the second theophany. He contrasted the church's trumpet blast with the Lord's glorious appearing. He contrasted the Lord's coming (*parousia*) with the end (*telos*). He contrasted the Lord coming to his spiritual temple with the second coming. And he contrasted the Lord coming to his spiritual temple with his entrance or appearance. There should be no doubt that he made a distinction between the rapture and the second coming that was both temporal and qualitative.

Two further theological evidences of his pretribulational position occur in his writings. The first is that several passages present the godly being removed and the ungodly being left behind to go through the time of judgment. A clear example of this is where he presents the church being delivered from coming judgment in the heavenly ark even as Noah was delivered from the flood in the earthly ark. This removal of the godly from among the ungodly only fits a pretribulation rapture. The exact opposite happens at the second coming when the ungodly are removed from the presence of the godly, and the godly are left to enter into the kingdom. This reverse order is seen, for instance, in the kingdom of heaven parables in Matthew chapter 13.

The second is that his amillennialism forced his hand on 1 Corinthians 15:22-24 — "Christ the firstfruits, afterward those that are Christ's at his coming, then the end" — and obligated him to apply *the end* to the second coming. He could not place it after the millennium because amillennialists reject a literal, earthly kingdom. But placing *the end* at the second coming obligated him to embrace a gathering of the church prior to the second coming. How so? Because the language of the passage makes a temporal distinction between the gathering and the end.

Now Eusebius' handling of this passage does not identify when and under what circumstances he believed that this gathering would occur. But he clearly teaches in other passages that the church shall be removed prior to the antichrist.

IRENAEUS

INTRODUCTORY OBSERVATIONS

Irenaeus is one of the earliest of the church fathers. He was born around AD 130 in Smyrna (modern Izmir, Turkey), spent many years as the bishop of Lugdumum (modern Lyon, France), and died around AD 202. He is honored by the church for having combated the heterodox notions of Gnosticism in his work *Against Heresies*. He was premillennial and pretribulational. His views on these eschatological matters are especially significant because he personally knew Polycarp and other aged men who had learned at the feet of the apostles.

IRENAEUS IS GROUND ZERO

In many ways, Irenaeus has become ground zero for the controversy regarding the rapture views of the early fathers. There are two reasons for this. First of all, his presentation on the events of the last days in the fifth book of his *Against Heresies* is the earliest extensive treatment of prophecy in the early church. Secondly, he had personally known associates of the apostles, like Polycarp, who was a disciple of the apostle John. He, in fact, claims that he obtained his prophetic views from the aged brothers who had interacted with the apostles. This is very significant. His proximity to the apostles implies that his sentiments on subjects like the rapture, Israel, and the tribulation are tantalizingly close to the sentiments of the apostles themselves.

This ground-zero dynamic has introduced an animated debate over the prophetic views of Irenaeus. The anti-dispensationalists cherry-pick him to find passages that "prove" that he taught a post-tribulation rapture like the later fathers did. The dispensationalists believe that they see evidence in his writings that he taught the same pretribulation rapture that they see in the Bible.

How can we know who is right? By the correct methodology, candor, and elbow grease. We must approach Irenaeus' *Against Heresies* with the same robust, consistent, impartial application of the historical-grammatical hermeneutic that we use (or should use) when we handle the word of God. And that is exactly what we aim to do in the following pages.

As the arguments unfold, it will become evident to unbiased readers that Irenaeus not only held to a pretribulation rapture but to four other salient features of dispensationalism: the distinction between the New Testament saints and the Old Testament saints (the latter being God's focus again in the tribulation), God's return to the people and nation of Israel, temple-observant Jews offering sacrifices in the tribulation, and two classes of saints in the millennium.

CONTRADICTION IN IRENAEUS?

The biggest difficulty we face in determining Irenaeus' view of the rapture is that, at first glance, he seems to be on both sides of the fence. For instance, in *Against Heresies 5.29.1*, he presents an apparent pretribulation rapture position when he locates the time of unprecedented tribulation after the catching up of the church.

> *And therefore, in the end, when the Church is suddenly caught up from this, it is said, "There shall be tribulation such as has not been since the beginning, neither shall be." For this is the last contest of the righteous, in which, when they overcome, they are crowned with incorruption.*

On the other hand, in *Against Heresies 5.26.1*, we find a statement that appears to teach a posttribulation rapture view. He clearly states that the antichrist shall put the church to flight during the tribulation.

> "And the ten horns which thou sawest are ten kings, who have received no kingdom as yet, but shall receive power as if kings one hour with the beast" ... And they shall lay Babylon waste, and burn her with fire, and shall give their kingdom to the beast, and put the Church to flight. After that, they shall be destroyed by the coming of our Lord.

Many prophecy students camp on this passage and claim that Irenaeus was indisputably a posttribulationist. They are shocked that anyone could believe that Irenaeus was a pretribulationist in the face of such clear testimony. Others, stumped by the apparent contradiction, conclude that Irenaeus' position was unclear.

THE CORRECT HANDLING OF TERMINOLOGY

At first glance, the above passage, *Against Heresies 5.26.1*, does look like incontrovertible proof that Irenaeus believed that the church would go through the tribulation. But all that glitters is not gold. This is true for those who prospect for real gold. It is also true for those who prospect for exegetical gold.

One of the first principles of exegesis (for both the Bible and historical pieces) is determining the author's intended meaning for the critical terms that he employs. To the degree that men fail to do this, they fail to rightly understand the author they are trying to interpret. When men drop the ball in this regard, the passage or work in question becomes a lackey for the expositor's prejudices.

This is precisely the situation that we have here. Men jump on the presence of the word *church*, assume that Irenaeus' use of *church* is identical to its use in modern evangelicalism, and conclude that Irenaeus taught a posttribulation rapture. But this assumption is wrong. We have a moral obligation to determine what Irenaeus meant when he used the word *church* and not merely assume that his use was identical to ours. If you don't understand his ecclesiology, you can't and won't understand his eschatology.

Anyone with even a modicum of understanding in the field of historical theology knows that the early church, the medieval church, and the Reformation churches often gave the word *church* a different meaning than dispensationalism does. Those in the dispensational camp limit the range of *church* to the redeemed of the current age (Pentecost to the rapture). The other theological persuasions often used *church* to refer to all the redeemed of all the ages. Those armed with this information enter into their investigation of Irenaeus knowing that he most likely used the word *church* differently than contemporary evangelicals who have been influenced by modern dispensational thought. They would not assume that his comment on the *church* in the tribulation proves that he believed that the saints of this age (Pentecost to the rapture) would go through the tribulation. They would investigate his comments on the meaning of *church* before they decided who he thought was going to be in the tribulation.

IRENAEUS' USE OF THE WORD "CHURCH" — TWO PROGRAMS

As it turns out, Irenaeus uses *church* in a sense that differs from how it is used in both the dispensational camp and in the posttribulational camp. He makes this clear in *Against Heresies* 5.34.1.

> *Now I have shown a short time ago that the church is the seed of Abraham; and for this reason, that we may know that he who in the* **New Testament** *"raises up from the stones children unto Abraham," is he who will gather, according to the* **Old Testament**, *those that shall be saved from all the nations. Jeremiah says: "Behold, the days come, saith the Lord, that they shall no more say, The Lord liveth, [who brought up the children of Israel out of the*

land of Egypt; But, the Lord liveth] who led the children of Israel from the north, and from every region whither they had been driven; he will restore them to their own land which he gave to their fathers."[12]

Two features of Irenaeus' ecclesiology jump off the page. First of all, he envisions two distinct redemption programs: the New Testament Gentile program and the OT Israel program, the latter including the Lord's return to Israel in the tribulation when he saves, gathers, and restores the nation of Israel according to the Old Testament promises. This is the same distinction between the church and Israel that is made by modern dispensationalism.

Secondly, he includes both of these programs — the saved Gentiles of the New Testament program and the saved tribulation Jews of the Old Testament program — under the heading *church*. He uses *church* for all the seed of Abraham, both the Gentile stones of this age (the spiritual seed) and the saved Jews of the tribulation (the physical seed).

Modern dispensationalism has no beef with the essence of this teaching. We hold the same concept of the general body of the redeemed of all ages, but we refer to this body by generic terms like the redeemed of all ages, the saints of all ages, and so forth. The difference between contemporary dispensationalism and Irenaeus on this point lies not in essence but in terminology. We limit the term *church* to those who are saved from Pentecost to the pretribulation rapture. Those saved during the tribulation we call tribulation saints, and those saved in the Old Testament we call Old Testament saints. Irenaeus uses *church* for all the seed of Abraham: both the Gentile stones of the New Testament era (the spiritual seed) and the saved Jews of the tribulation era (the physical seed).

But there is an insurmountable difference between Irenaeus' two-program view and posttribulationism. No one in that camp believes that God returns to national Israel as his people during the seventieth week. They all believe that the church of this age will enter into the tribulation and that the church-age economy will continue until the second coming.

IRENAEUS TEACHES TWO CHURCHES

Another passage that sheds light on what Irenaeus meant when he used the word *church* is found in *Against Heresies, 4.31.1-2.*[13]

> *As says the Scripture, "And that night the elder went in and lay with her father, and Lot knew not when she lay down, nor when she arose." And the same thing took place in the case of the younger ... the arrangement [designed by God] was carried out, by which the two daughters (that is,* **the two synagogues***), who gave to children begotten of one and the same father, were pointed out ...* **the elder and the younger synagogues ... the two synagogues, that is, the two churches,**[14] *produced from their own father living sons to the living God.*

The *elder synagogue* is clearly a reference to the Jewish saints of the Old Testament era, and the *younger synagogue* is clearly a reference to the Gentile saints of the New Testament era. These statements force us to the conclusion that Irenaeus viewed Israel and the Gentile believers of this age as distinct churches, that is, distinct bodies of believers. This is the same distinction that contemporary dispensationalism makes, though we differ in terminology. Speaking in a general sense, we can agree with the concept of two churches. But speaking in a technical sense, we refer to these two bodies as Israel and the church.

Now Irenaeus' handling of the word *church* here speaks volumes on what he meant when he spoke of the *church* in the tribulation under the antichrist (*Against Heresies 5.26.1*). The *church* in the tribulation there could be either a reference to the Old Testament church or to the New Testament church. The passage in and of itself is not conclusive. It must be interpreted in the light of other passages in his works that shed light on the subject of the tribulation and who it is that languishes therein.

GOD'S RETURN TO ISRAEL

In the same chapter where he taught the distinction between the Old Testament seed and the New Testament seed, *Against Heresies, 5.34.1*, Irenaeus also taught the regathering and restoration of Israel.

> *He who in the New Testament* **"raises up** *from the stones children unto Abraham," is He who* **will gather,** *according to the Old Testament,* ***those that shall be saved*** *from all the nations, Jeremiah says: "Behold, the days come, saith the Lord, that they shall no more say, The Lord liveth, [who brought up the children of Israel out of the land of Egypt; But, the Lord liveth] who led the children of Israel from the north, and from every region whither they had been driven; He will restore them to their own land which He gave to their fathers."*[15]

Notice the use of the present tense *raises up* when addressing God's work in building the Gentile church of this age and the use of the future tense *will gather* and *shall be saved* when addressing God's work with the people and nation of Israel in the last days. This is making a temporal distinction between God's work with the church and his work with Israel. The church IS God's program on earth now. Israel SHALL BE God's program on earth in the future during the tribulation.

Notice further that those saved from the nations is not a reference to Gentiles being saved but to the scattered Jews being saved. In the last days after the rapture of the church, Jews who have been scattered among the nations through many painful seasons of tribulation and persecution will be saved. These saved Jews will be gathered back to the land of Israel at the second coming. This is the obvious intent of the prophecy in Jeremiah, and there is zero reason to believe that Irenaeus took it in any sense other than strictly literal.

In the same chapter, Irenaeus also quotes Ezekiel on this matter, further affirming his belief in the salvation and restoration of literal Israel in the last days.

> *"Behold, I will open your tombs and bring you forth out of your graves ... and I will put breath in you, and you shall live; and I will place you on your own land, and you shall know that I am the Lord ...* **I will gather Israel from all nations whither they have been driven, and I shall be sanctified in them in the sight of the sons of the nations: and they shall dwell in their own land, which I gave to my servant Jacob.** *... I shall cause judgment to fall among all who have dishonoured them, among those who encircle them round about; and they shall know that I am the Lord their God, and the God of their fathers."*

Notice what it is that Irenaeus is affirming. At the time of the resurrection of the godly Israelites and the destruction of the nations gathered against Israel, the Lord will gather the Jews from every nation where they were scattered and bring them to their own land. This implies the salvation of these Jews as Jews during the tribulation.

JEWS IN THE TRIBULATION

In several passages Irenaeus portrays an Israel-focus in the tribulation, presenting the temple and temple service as God-honored and identifying the saints as Jewish believers. For instance, in *Against Heresies 5.25.4,* he presents Jewish believers who offer pure sacrifices to God.

> *A king of a most fierce countenance shall arise ... then he points out the time that his tyranny shall last, during which the saints shall be put to flight, they who offer a pure sacrifice unto God: "And in the midst of the week," he says, "the sacrifice and the libation shall be taken away, and the abomination of desolation [shall be brought] into the temple: even unto the consummation of the time shall*

the desolation be complete." Now three years and six months constitute the half-week.

Notice that he qualifies *saints* here with the expression, "they who offer a pure sacrifice to God." Notice further that the phrase "pure sacrifice" refers to offering literal sacrifices in the literal temple. This language unequivocally informs us that Irenaeus believed that in the tribulation saved Jews will offer temple sacrifices that will be honored by God.

In a similar vein in *Against Heresies 5.28.2*, he identifies the defiled temple as the temple of God.

> *For when he (Antichrist) is come, and of his own accord concentrates in his own person the apostasy ... sitting also in the temple of God,*[16] *so that his dupes may adore him as the Christ [annointed one] ... "and blasphemy and power was given to him during forty and two months. And he opened his mouth for blasphemy against God, to blaspheme His name and His tabernacle, and those who dwell in heaven ... Here is the endurance and the faith of the saints."*[17]

Notice that Irenaeus refers to the physical temple in Jerusalem as THE temple of God. Notice too that he, with the Scriptures, places blaspheming God's tabernacle in the same category as blaspheming God himself, or God's Son, or God's redeemed in heaven. This implies that he recognizes God's ownership of the temple during the time of tribulation. Moreover, this connection to the temple implies that the tribulation saints referred to are Jewish believers.[18]

Now Irenaeus' perspective in the above passages on the tribulation economy has monumental consequences for the rapture question. If he has saved men during the seventieth week offering pure sacrifices that are acceptable to God in a temple owned by God, then he believed in a pretribulation rapture, and he believed that God will return to Israel during the seventieth week to finish up the last seven years of his Jewish program which he foretold in Daniel 9:24-27.

A PRETRIBULATION RAPTURE OF THE SAINTS

Not only does Irenaeus portray the tribulation saints as practicing Jews whose temple service is honored by God, but he also portrays the Gentile saints of the present age as being caught up from this defiled realm before the tribulation starts. This pretribulational conviction is presented in four distinct passages which we shall examine in turn. One of them is fairly well-known in pretribulation circles. The other three have gone largely unnoticed.

The first is *Against Heresies 5.29.1*, which is already familiar to many students of prophecy. Here we find a clear statement that the rapture will precede the time of tribulation.

> *And therefore in the end when the Church is suddenly caught up from this, it is said, "There shall be tribulation such as has not been since the beginning, neither shall be." For this is the last contest of the righteous, in which, when they overcome, they are crowned with incorruption.*

Notice the grammatical structure. "When the church is suddenly caught up" is a circumstantial clause that tells us the circumstance upon which the action of the main verb hinges. The main verb is "there shall be tribulation." Notice that the action is couched in the future tense. This places the tribulation after the rapture. WHEN the sudden catching up of the church startles the world, THEN there shall be tribulation. There is no way under the sun that this sentence can mean that the tribulation precedes the rapture.

The force of the grammar in the English translation cannot be vacated by appealing to the Latin translation behind the English. The Latin says, cum ... Ecclesia assumetur, erit tribulatio, "when the church is caught up, there shall be tribulation." Here again, the use of the future verb form erit "there shall be" presents the tribulation as following the rapture.

Nor does referring to the original Greek change anything. The Greek says, τῆς ἐκκλησίας ἀναλαμβανομένης, ἔσται, φησίν, θλῖψις, "when the church is caught up, there shall be tribulation." Once again, the tribulation is grammatically connected to the preceding circumstance with the future tense "there shall be tribulation." This informs us that the tribulation follows the rapture.

In *Against Heresies 5.5.1*, we find Enoch's translation presented as an illustration of the rapture.

> *For Enoch, when he pleased God, was translated in the same body in which he did please Him, thus pointing out by anticipation the translation of the just. ... Wherefore also the elders who were disciples of the apostles tell us that those who are translated are translated to that place (for paradise has been prepared for righteous men, such as have the Spirit; in which place also Paul the apostle, when he was caught up, heard unspeakable words...), and that those who have been translated shall remain there until the consummation [the end], as a prelude to incorruptibility.*

Notice the flow of thought here. Enoch was translated to glory before the arrival of sweeping judgment on earth. His translation is a type of the rapture of the church prior to judgment. In the days of Irenaeus, there were aged men yet alive, like Polycarp, who had been disciples of the apostles themselves. These patriarchs taught a coming translation event that would transport men to heaven where they would remain until the end of the age. In other words, they would be delivered from the coming judgment even as Enoch was delivered from the coming flood. This translation will bless the church with a prelude to the incorruptibility that shall be introduced at the second coming. Irenaus' teaching, then, on the translation of the church prior to judgment is a pretribulation rapture.

Another pretribulation rapture testimony is found in *Against Heresies 5.31.2* where Irenaeus' treatment resembles that in John 14:1-3.

> *For as the Lord "went away in the midst of the shadow of death," where the souls of the dead were, yet afterwards arose in the body, and after the resurrection was taken up, it is manifest that the souls of His disciples also, upon whose account the Lord underwent these things, shall go away into the invisible place allotted to them by God, and there remain until the resurrection, awaiting that event; then receiving their bodies, and rising in their entirety, that is bodily, just as the Lord arose, they shall come thus into the presence of God.*

Notice that Irenaeus does not portray the church staying down here on earth at the time of the resurrection, which is what he would portray if he were presenting the posttribulation rapture understanding. Rather, he portrays the church rising into the presence of God. This translation to heaven — a recurring theme in his eschatology — exudes the same spirit as John 14:1-3. The next time the church engages bodily with the Lord, those asleep in Jesus will rise from the dead, then the church entire will embark, not on a sideways journey to another location on earth, but on a vertical journey to the third heaven, even the New Jerusalem. This journey implies a pretribulation rapture. The church rises to heaven, then stays there until the time of the second coming.

Yet another pretribulation rapture testimony in this regard appears in *Against Heresies 5.32.1*.

> *But it is necessary to say on these things, that it behoves the righteous to be the first in this condition which is being renewed, rising up to the appearance (visible observation) of God to receive the promise of inheritance which God promised to the fathers: afterward to be a judge.*

Notice that in Irenaeus's estimation, the church is the first to receive the renewed condition, which implies that he believes that others will receive the same renewing at a later time. This agrees with his statement above that the rapture of the church will be a prelude to the full program of incorruptibility at the second coming. Also, take notice once again of his focus on the upward rise to the visible presence of God. The journey to heaven implies a pretribulation rapture. Finally, observe that Irenaeus sees the church first rising to receive her promised inheritance, then afterwards engaging in her work in the office of judge here on earth. This clearly distinguishes the rapture of the church and the church's return at the second coming to rule with Christ down here on earth.

These passages are decisive. Irenaeus taught that the church ascends to heaven at the rapture, stays there until the end of the age, and receives the resurrection renewal before the wholesale renewal at the second coming. He also makes a clear temporal distinction between the church receiving her reward and the church operating in the office of judge. These points force us to conclude that Irenaeus adhered to a pretribulation rapture.

TWO CLASSES OF SAINTS IN THE KINGDOM

The final line of dispensational thought that we see in Irenaeus is that he held to two classes of saints in the kingdom. This point is clearly made in *Against Heresies, 5.35.1*.

> *The resurrection of the just, which happens after the coming of Antichrist and the destruction of all nations under his rule; when the righteous shall reign in the earth ... those whom the Lord shall find in the flesh, awaiting Him from heaven, and who have suffered tribulation and escaped the hands of the wicked one. For it is in reference to them that the prophet says: "And the remnant shall multiply upon the earth." And as many believers as God has prepared for this purpose, for a remnant multiplying*

upon earth, shall also be UNDER *the rule of the saints to serve this Jerusalem, and [His] kingdom shall be in it.*

Notice the two classes. The first is the tribulation saints, described by Irenaeus as "those whom the Lord shall find in the flesh, awaiting him from heaven, who have suffered tribulation and escaped the hands of the wicked one." These saints will multiply upon the earth.

The second is the ruling class of saints. Notice the language. "As many believers as the Lord has prepared for this purpose, for a remnant multiplying upon earth, SHALL BE UNDER THE RULE OF THE SAINTS." So the ruling class of saints rules over the tribulation saints. This ruling class can only be the glorified church that descends with Christ at the second coming who shall sit in Christ's throne with him.

While Irenaeus doesn't employ the terminology favored by modern dispensationalism — the tribulation saints and the church saints — yet the distinction he makes is identical to that made by them. And in matters of this kind, substance is vastly more important than terminology.

IRENAEUS' DISPENSATIONALISM

In the preceding pages, we have seen that Irenaeus taught five core tenets of dispensationalism — a distinction between the Gentile saints of the current age and the Jewish saints of the tribulation, the rapture of the church prior to the tribulation, God's return to national Israel for salvation and blessing, Jewish saints in the tribulation who practice temple service that is honored of God, and two classes of saints in the kingdom — the unglorified and the glorified.

This is explosive evidence in the debate concerning the rapture views of the early fathers on two levels. First of all, this is not merely a stray passage that appears to teach a pretribulation rapture. This is a developed dispensational system that presents the same core teachings that modern dispensationalism teaches.

Secondly, Irenaeus' proximity to the apostles is extremely provocative. He claims that he got his prophetic views from the aged men, like Polycarp, who personally interacted with the apostles. This establishes the claim by dispensationalists, based on the teaching of the Bible and the apostles, that the pretribulation rapture was the view of the earliest fathers.

But the pretribulation rapture teaching faced an existential threat almost from the beginning. In the second century, not far removed from the apostles, men began drinking from the heady fountain of allegorical hermeneutics and replacement theology. Teachers as early as Irenaeus felt obliged to oppose the evil of taking the Old Testament prophecies allegorically.[19] This system wrenched the millennium and the tribulation out of the category of Jewish prophecy and placed them in the category of Christian experience. The millennium was the first to vanish in the wasteland of allegorical hermeneutics, being largely expelled by the time of Augustine and Jerome. The pretribulation rapture hung on somewhat longer, particularly in the Eastern (the Antiochian or Syrian) school. But eventually, the tribulation too was stolen from Israel and handed over to the church. This was, obviously, the death of the pretribulation rapture.

May Irenaeus' robust dispensational testimony help reverse the devastation caused by replacement theology, both the full-fledged version that is advanced by amillennialism and the partial version that is taught by posttribulationism.

THE DIDACHE

INTRODUCTORY OBSERVATIONS

When considering the eschatological beliefs of the early church, one of the documents that absolutely must be considered is the *Didache*, also known as *The Teaching of the Twelve*. Though some scholars date this document in the early second century, most commonly it is dated in the first century, generally AD 70 to AD 100. This puts it in competition for the earliest Christian document outside of the New Testament books. It may have been written while the apostle John was still alive and the canon of Scripture was not yet completed — i.e. the book of Revelation was not yet penned.

Whether an individual or a group of men penned this work is unknown. But the author or authors had undoubtedly known the apostolic associates, and probably the apostles themselves. This is provocative information. Irenaeus was one chain link removed from the apostles. The authors of the Didache were even closer. They had one foot in the apostolic era. Their views on the rapture, then, could be expected to reflect the apostles' view on the rapture.

A ROBUST PROPHETIC PASSAGE

The final section of the document, Section 16, zeroes in on the subject of the last days, covering the rapture, the tribulation, the antichrist, and the second coming.

Watch for your life's sake. Let not your lamps be quenched, nor your loins unloosed; but be ready, for you know not the hour in which our Lord will come. But come together often, seeking the things which are befitting to your souls: for the whole time of your faith will not profit you, if you are not made perfect in the last time. For in the last days false prophets and corrupters shall be multiplied, and the sheep shall be turned into wolves, and love shall be turned into hate; for when lawlessness increases, they shall hate and persecute and betray one another, and then shall appear the world-deceiver as Son of God, and shall do signs and wonders, and the earth shall be delivered into his hands, and he shall do iniquitous things which have never yet come to pass since the beginning. Then shall the creation of men come into the fire of trial, and many shall be made to stumble and shall perish; but those who endure in their faith shall be saved from under the curse itself. And then shall appear the signs of the truth: first, the sign of an outspreading in heaven, then the sign of the sound of the trumpet. And third, the resurrection of the dead — yet not of all, but as it is said: "The Lord shall come and all His saints with Him." Then shall the world see the Lord coming upon the clouds of heaven.

This brief passage presents three distinct arguments for a pretribulation rapture: the classic imminence argument, the choice between glorification or tribulation, and the already resurrected church returning with the Lord at the second coming. We will walk through each of these arguments in turn.

THE FIRST RAPTURE ARGUMENT

The **first** argument is the well-known and straightforward imminence passage.

Watch for your life's sake. Let not your lamps be quenched, nor your loins unloosed; but be ready, for you know not the hour in which our Lord will come.

This is a strong argument for the pretribulation rapture from the angle of imminence. How so? Because the phrase "you know not the hour" doesn't fit the second coming. It does, however, fit the rapture admirably.

This is simply a matter of understanding the day of the Lord. This prophetic day bears a strong analogy to a normal day. The normal day has four aspects: the morning star, the dawning, the sunrise, and the day proper. So with the coming day of the Lord. The rapture is the morning star of the day of the Lord (Rev. 2:28, Rev. 22:16, 2 Pe 1:19). The tribulation is the dawning of the day (1 Thess. 5:1-5). The second coming is the sunrise of the day (Mal. 4:1-3). The kingdom is the actual day of the Lord in contrast to man's day. Bearing this analogy in mind, when we read about the coming of the Lord or the day of the Lord in any particular prophetic passage in the Bible, we must determine which of these four aspects is in view.

In the Irenaeus passage above, it is obviously not the sunrise aspect, the second coming proper, that is under consideration. The phrase "you know not the hour" doesn't fit that aspect. As men can count the minutes from nautical dawn or civil dawn to sunrise, so men will be able to reckon the time of the second coming. Once the antichrist forces his treaty upon Israel, men know the exact date of the start of the seventieth week. From there, calculating the time of the second coming is a matter of elementary-school math. They just need to count the days — seven years of 360 days each. Ditto for counting from the middle of the seventieth week when the antichrist sits in the temple, declares himself God, and demands worship on pain of death. They just need to count 1260 days.

But not knowing the hour fits the rapture admirably. The rapture, as the morning star, is the first hint of the approaching day of the Lord. As the morning star sneaks up on the world unnoticed and without warning, coming before any other sign of the dawning of the day, so the rapture will sneak up on the world unnoticed and without prior warning. Once a man notices the morning star, he knows that dawn is near. So it is with the rapture. Once it happens, the world knows, or should know at any rate, that the dawning of the day of the Lord is upon them.

THE SECOND RAPTURE ARGUMENT

The **second** argument follows on the heels of the exhortation to watch and not let their lamps go out. There we read,

> *But come together often, seeking the things which are befitting to your souls: for the whole time of your faith will not profit you, if you are not made perfect in the last time.*

The phrase *made perfect* is the Greek verb *teleioō* in the passive. This verb, when used in last-days contexts, is more or less equivalent to our *glorified* and constitutes a reference to the resurrection. [The evidence for this will be given at the end of this chapter.] For the church, of course, the resurrection and rapture are one and the same. Wherever the resurrection happens, there the rapture happens.

We conclude, then, that the sentence "the whole time of your faith will not profit you if you are not *made perfect* in the last time" is a warning that professing Christians need to make sure that they are not left behind when the rapture happens. We could paraphrase this sentence as "The whole time of your church going will gain you nothing if you are not raptured."

This rapture warning is followed by a terse description of the horrors of the tribulation that men will face if they are left behind.

> *For in the last days false prophets and corrupters shall be multiplied, and the sheep shall be turned into wolves ... and then shall appear the world-deceiver as Son of God, and shall do signs and wonders, and the earth shall be delivered into his hands, and he shall do iniquitous things*

which have never yet come to pass since the beginning. Then shall the creation of men come into the fire of trial.

Notice that the word *for*. This little workhorse points to explanations and reasons. Here the horrors of the tribulation are given as the reason why professing Christians need to make sure that they do not miss the rapture.

The gist of the argument, then, is that men have a choice: glorification or tribulation. They can go up in the rapture or go through the tribulation. This choice is very similar to the choice contemporary preachers lay before men: heaven or hell, rapture or tribulation, rapture or wrath. Once we understand the choice, the warning becomes clear. Don't play games. Don't dabble. Don't settle for mere religion. Don't just be a churchgoer. Test yourself and make sure you are of the faith. Make sure you are born again. Don't be left behind. You don't want to miss the rapture and go through the tribulation. Mere dabblers in Christianity will not be glorified but will be left behind to go into the tribulation and face the greatest display of satanic iniquity on earth since the beginning of time.

THE THIRD RAPTURE ARGUMENT

The **third** argument is the partial resurrection at the second coming. At the end of the section we read,

And then shall appear the signs of the truth: first, the sign of an outspreading in heaven, then the sign of the sound of the trumpet. And third, the resurrection of the dead — yet not of all, indeed as it is said: "The Lord shall come and all his saints with him." Then shall the world see the Lord coming upon the clouds of heaven.

Notice the phrase "yet not all" spoken in regard to the resurrection. The phrase is not a reference to the distinction between the resurrection of the just and the resurrection of the unjust. How do we know this? Because the context clarifies what is meant. The limiting statement "yet not all" is followed by the clarifying statement, "The Lord shall come and all His saints with Him."

The "yet not all" means that only the Old Testament saints and the tribulation martyrs will be raised at the second coming. The church was already raised at the rapture prior to the tribulation — in keeping with the promise in Revelation 3:10 that the Lord will keep the church from the hour of trial.

The additional thought, "The Lord shall come and all his saints with him," means that the already glorified church shall accompany the Lord at the second coming when he descends to trample the wine press at Armageddon and establish his kingdom.

This is amazing. Here we have clear evidence that the first-century church owned the dispensational position that the Lord will descend from heaven twice in the last days: once for the church and once with the church. Once before the tribulation and once after the tribulation.

THE DIDACHE'S ESCHATOLOGY

So we see that three distinct arguments for a pretribulation rapture — all used by pretribulationists today — are made in one brief passage in the Didache: the classic imminence argument, the choice between glorification and tribulation, and the already glorified church descending with the Lord at the second coming. This three-strand cord will not be easily broken. It constitutes forceful, indisputable evidence that the pretribulation rapture was held in the early church, by men with one foot in the apostolic era.

But we find more than a pretribulation rapture here. We find many of the hallmarks of a robust dispensational (literal) handling of the prophetic Scriptures: a left-behind warning, a literal tribulation, a literal antichrist, tribulation saints, a distinction between the rapture and the second coming, and two phases in the resurrection (those raised at the second coming and those raised in the rapture who come with the Lord at the second coming). The Didache, as can be seen, packs a tremendous amount of prophetic teaching into one succinct paragraph. It is one of the densest prophetic passages to be found in all of the patristic literature.

THE USE OF TELEIOŌ FOR THE GLORIFICATION OF THE RESURRECTION

In the following passages gleaned from the early fathers, the Greek verb τελειόω (teleioō) *perfect* or *complete* is used in resurrection contexts. These contexts demonstrate that *made perfect* in such prophetic contexts is more or less equivalent to the English *glorified*.

This prophetic usage of the term *teleioō* is one of five main uses in patristic literature involving Christian experience. These uses string together like heavenly pearls to adorn the believer.

ONE — Completeness as a human being when born again
TWO — Maturity (completeness) as a believer
THREE — Spiritual strength completed (fulfilled) in weakness
FOUR — Completion of one's assigned work or mission
FIVE — Completion (glorification) in the resurrection

Theodore of Cyrus, Interpretation in the Fourteen Epistles of Saint Paul, 1 Thess. 4:16, (Migne, vol. 82, p. 649)

> This is stated in the epistle to the Hebrews. "All these made perfect through faith have not obtained the promises in the holy apostle, God having provided something better for us, that they should not be **made perfect** apart from us." Therefore, all the godly together shall be brightened (glorified), the FIRST to enjoy the resurrection. For this he [Paul] also teaches in the epistle to the Corinthians. "Christ the first fruits, then those who are Christ's at his coming, then the end."

Notice that the second *made perfect* in Hebrews 11:40 is associated with the resurrection, a connection made almost universally by modern evangelicals. Notice too that the glorious change is described as being brightened or glorified.

Theodore of Cyrus, Interpretation in the Fourteen Epistles of Saint Paul, Hebrews 11:39-40, (Migne, vol. 82, p. 769)

> *"All these all having obtained a good report through faith have not obtained the promise, God having provided something better for us, that they should not be **made perfect** apart from us." So although their battles have been many and great, yet still they do not yet enjoy their crowns (victory wreaths).*

In Theodore's eyes, the saints receive their promises and crowns on the same day that they are made perfect. This can only be the day of the resurrection, which for the church is the rapture.

Eusebius, Fragments in Luke, Migne, vol. 24, p. 561

> *But he promises at the end to increase and **perfect** them, take them up, and bring them into his bridal chamber, where he will recline them (set them relaxed at his table) and serve them.*

Notice the use of the rapture terminology *take them up* (*paralambanō*) which is followed by a clear statement that they are going to the bridal chamber. This is clearly a rapture reference. At the time of the rapture, the church will be increased and perfected (glorified).

Methodius, Life of Euthymius of Sardinia, 25

> *But when they shall outrise [from the dead] and shall outshine the sun, whatever they were promised, then the whole promise they shall obtain and this not apart from anyone but with everyone they shall **be perfected**.*

Methodius associates perfection (glorification) with the resurrection, and he adds that those who enjoy this glorification privilege will outshine the sun.

Origen, Against Celsus, 4.29

*And we know that in this way the angels are superior to men; so that men, when **made perfect**, become like the angels. For in the resurrection of the dead, they neither marry nor are given in marriage, but the righteous are as the angels in heaven, and also become equal to the angels.*

Origen clearly associates obtaining *perfection* (glorification) with the resurrection of the righteous dead. This glorification will change them to be like the angels.

Athanasius, Questions in Sacred Scripture, Migne, vol. 28, p. 772

*For this is what the apostle said, that "God having provided something better for us, that they should not be **made perfect** apart from us." For apart from all the saints the half shall not receive the promised blessings. They have not yet received **the [promised] perfection**, for this is better, that all shall enter into the kingdom at the same time (in the same season), and from equality (on the same [ground]), all the saints shall receive the blessings of God.*

Athanasius equates the blessings of the resurrection with the concept of glorification, expressing this wonderful change with both the passive verb and the noun.

Ephraim the Syrian, How the Thief Entered Paradise Before the Resurrection, Phrantzolas, vol. 7

Because it is not yet the time of the reward for our labors. For the apostle says concerning the righteous, "These all having obtained a good report through faith have not obtained the promise, God having provided something *better for us, that they should not be **made perfect** apart from us."*

Ephraim clearly associates perfection (glorification) with the time of reward for our labors, which all happily confess to be the time of the church's resurrection.

Conclusion

Strong evidence was presented in this volume, via the Didache and Irenaeus, that there was a clear dispensational testimony in the first two centuries of the church. Further strong evidence was presented, via Eusebius and Ephraim, that there was a clear pretribulational testimony in the fourth century, despite the efforts of the heavyweights in Christendom to force the allegorical methodology and replacement theology upon the entire church.

We do not, of course, forward these patristic passages as proof that the pretribulation rapture is true. The Bible alone is the only rule of faith and practice. On this ground, we live and die. In its pages we find an ironclad case for a pretribulation rapture with promises like the church being kept from the hour of trial which shall come upon the whole world (Rev. 3:10), the church being gathered prior to the day of the Lord (2 Thess. 2:1-3), and the rewarded church appearing in heaven prior to the opening of the first seal (Rev. 4-5).

On the contrary, the only reason we forward these passages is to overthrow the often-repeated claim that the pretribulation rapture is a new doctrine that was introduced by J. N. Darby in 1830 after he learned it from a demon-possessed young lady by the name of Margaret MacDonald, who was a prophetess in the Irvingite movement. This is an outrageous fabrication, as anyone who honestly examines the evidence can see for himself.

First of all, the pretribulation rapture is not a new doctrine. It was believed by many in the early church, as we demonstrated in this volume. But the blessed hope was swept from the church by a relentless tsunami of replacement theology beginning in the third century. Happily, the return to sola Scriptura in the Reformation led to the recovery of this precious truth. Many men and women taught or proposed a pretribulation rapture before Darby, a rapture that would happen prior to the time of judgment and would be temporally distinct from the second coming.[20]

Secondly, Darby did not get his understanding of the rapture from Margaret MacDonald. She taught a rapture that would happen after three and a half years of tribulation under the antichrist. This is, for all practical purposes, a prewrath rapture. She received this teaching in 1830 from a spirit pretending to be the Holy Spirit.[21] Darby taught a pretribulation rapture that would occur prior to the antichrist and his reign of iniquity. He was convinced of this view by the Greek of 2 Thessalonians 2:3 in 1827, three years before Margaret's revelation.[22]

APPENDIX

EPHRAIM'S GREEK WORKS THAT WERE EXAMINED

The author read about half of these works in their entirety. For the other half, only the portions relating to the rapture or the tribulation were read. These portions were located by searching for the known eschatological terms used by Ephraim.

1) On the Destruction of Pride
Latin title: Ad eversionem superbiae
Greek title: Πρὸς καθαίρεσιν ὑπερηφανίας
Work ID: Roger Pearse #3, TLG #3
K.G. Phrantzolas, Ὁσίου Ἐφραίμ τοῦ Σύρου ἔργα, vol. 1, To Perivoli tis Panagias, 1988 (repr. 1995): 84-95.

2) Admonitory Message
Latin title: Sermo compunctorius
Greek title: Λόγος κατανυκτικός
Work ID: Roger Pearse #4, TLG #4
K.G. Phrantzolas, Ὁσίου Ἐφραίμ τοῦ Σύρου ἔργα, vol. 1, To Perivoli tis Panagias, 1988 (repr. 1995): 96-121.

3) Message on Asceticism
Latin title: Sermo asceticus
Greek title: Λόγος ασκητικός
Work ID: Roger Pearse #5, TLG #5
K.G. Phrantzolas, Ὁσίου Ἐφραίμ τοῦ Σύρου ἔργα, vol. 1, To Perivoli tis Panagias, 1988 (repr. 1995): 122-184.

4) On Repentance
Latin title: De paenitentia
Greek title: Περὶ μετανοίας
Work ID: Roger Pearse #11, TLG #10
K.G. Phrantzolas, Ὁσίου Ἐφραίμ τοῦ Σύρου ἔργα, vol. 1, To Perivoli tis Panagias, 1988 (repr. 1995): 362-374.

5) Hortatory Message
Latin title: Sermo paraeneticus
Greek title: Λόγος παραινετικός
Work ID: Roger Pearse #15, TLG #14
K.G. Phrantzolas, Ὁσίου Ἐφραίμ τοῦ Σύρου ἔργα, vol. 1, To Perivoli tis Panagias, 1988 (repr. 1995): 400-412.

6) On the Fathers Who Have Completed Their Course
Latin title: Sermo alius in patres defunctos
Greek title: Λόγος εἰς πατέρας τελειωθέντας
Work ID: Roger Pearse #16, TLG #15
K.G. Phrantzolas, Ὁσίου Ἐφραίμ τοῦ Σύρου ἔργα, vol. 2, To Perivoli tis Panagias, 1989: 9-16.

7) Another Sermon on the Fathers Who Completed Their Course
Latin title: Sermo in patres defunctos
Greek title: Λόγος ἕτερος εἰς πατέρας τελειωθέντας
Work ID: Roger Pearse #17, TLG #16
K.G. Phrantzolas, Ὁσίου Ἐφραίμ τοῦ Σύρου ἔργα, vol. 2, To Perivoli tis Panagias, 1989: 17-28.

8) The Fear of Souls
Latin title: De timore animarum
Greek title: Περὶ φόβου ψυχῶν
Work ID: Roger Pearse #20, TLG #19
K.G. Phrantzoles, Ὁσίου Ἐφραίμ τοῦ Σύρου ἔργα, vol. 2, To Perivoli tis Panagias, 1989: 34-43.

9) Reminder or Letter
Latin title: Hypmnesticon, sive epistula
Greek Title: Ὑπομνηστικόν, ἤτοι επιστολή
Work ID: Roger Pearse 22, TLG 21
K.G. Phrantzolas, Ὁσίου Ἐφραίμ τοῦ Σύρου ἔργα, vol. 2, To Perivoli tis Panagias, 1989: 46-58.

10) How the Soul Should Pray God with Tears
Latin title: Quomodo anima cum lacrymis debeat orare deum, quando tentatur ab inimico
Greek title: Περὶ ψυχῆς ὅταν πειράζηται ὑπὸ τοῦ Ἐχθροῦ πῶς ὀφείλει μετὰ δακρύων τῷ Θεῷ προσεύχεσθαι
Work ID: Roger Pearse #23, TLG #22.
K.G. Phrantzolas, Ὁσίου Ἐφραίμ τοῦ Σύρου ἔργα, vol. 2, To Perivoli tis Panagias, 1989: 59-70.

11) Fifty-Five Beatitudes
Latin title: Beatitudines, capita quinquaginta quinque
Greek title: Μακαρισμοί, κεφάλαια νε΄
Work ID: Roger Pearse #30, TLG #29
K.G. Phrantzolas, Ὁσίου Ἐφραίμ τοῦ Σύρου ἔργα, vol. 2, To Perivoli tis Panagias, 1989: 252-266.

12) Other Beatitudes, Twenty Chapters
Latin title: Beatitudines aliae, capita viginti
Greek title: Μακαρισμοί ἕτεροι, κεφάλαια κ΄
Work ID: Roger Pearse #31, TLG #32
K.G. Phrantzolas, Ὁσίου Ἐφραίμ τοῦ Σύρου ἔργα, vol. 2, To Perivoli tis Panagias, 1989: 267-279.

13) Hortatory Sermons to the Monks of Egypt
Latin title: Sermones paraenetici ad monachos Aegypti
Greek title: Λόγοι παραινετικοὶ πρὸς τοὺς κατ' Αἴγυπτον μοναχούς
Work ID: Roger Pearse, #37, TLG #36
K.G. Phrantzolas, Ὁσίου Ἐφραίμ τοῦ Σύρου ἔργα, vol. 3, To Perivoli tis Panagias, 1990: 36-294.

14) On the Blessed and the Cursed
Latin title: De beatitudinibus atque infelicitatibus
Greek title: Περὶ μακαρισμῶν καὶ ταλανισμῶν
Work ID: Roger Pearse #41, TLG #40
K.G. Phrantzolas, Ὁσίου Ἐφραίμ τοῦ Σύρου ἔργα, vol. 3, To Perivoli tis Panagias, 1990: 323-326.

15) On The Second Coming of Our Lord Jesus Christ
Latin title: In secundum adventum domini nostri Jesu Christi
Greek title: Εἰς τὴν δευτέραν παρουσίαν τοῦ Κυρίου ἡμῶν Ἰησοῦ Χριστοῦ
Work ID: Roger Pearse #49, TLG #48
K.G. Phrantzolas, Ὁσίου Ἐφραίμ τοῦ Σύρου ἔργα, vol. 3, To Perivoli tis Panagias, 1990: 404-415.

16) Sermon on the Second Coming of our Lord Jesus Christ
Latin title: Sermon in secundum adventum domini nostri Jesu Christi
Greek title: Λόγος εις της Δευτέραν Παρουσίαν του Κυρίου ημών Ιησού Χριστού
Work ID: Roger Pearse #50, TLG #49
K.G. Phrantzolas, Ὁσίου Ἐφραίμ τοῦ Σύρου ἔργα, vol. 4, To Perivoli tis Panagias, 1992: 9-46.

17) Sermon on the Common Resurrection, on repentance and love, and on the Second Coming of our Lord Jesus Christ

Latin title: Sermo de communi resurrectione, de paenitentia et de caritate, et in secundum adventum domini nostri Jesu Christi

Greek title: Λόγος περὶ τῆς κοινῆς ἀναστάσεως καὶ μετανοίας καὶ ἀγάπης. Καὶ εἰς τὴν δευτέραν παρουσίαν τοῦ Κυρίου ἡμῶν Ἰησοῦ Χριστοῦ

Work ID: Roger Pearse #51, TLG #50

K.G. Phrantzolas, Ὁσίου Ἐφραίμ τοῦ Σύρου ἔργα, vol. 4, Το Perivoli tis Panagias, 1992: 47-75.

18) Sermon on the Advent of the Lord, and the End of the Age, and the Coming of the Antichrist

Latin title: Sermo in adventum domini, et de consummatione saeculi, et in adventum antichristi

Greek title: Λόγος εἰς τὴν παρουσίαν τοῦ Κυρίου, καὶ περὶ συντελείας τοῦ κόσμου, καὶ εἰς τὴν παρουσίαν τοῦ Ἀντιχρίστου

Work ID: Roger Pearse #53, TLG #52

K.G. Phrantzolas, Ὁσίου Ἐφραίμ τοῦ Σύρου ἔργα, vol. 4, Το Perivoli tis Panagias, 1992: 111-128.

19) Sermon on the Valuable and Life-Giving Cross, and on the Second Coming, and on Love and Charity

Latin title: Sermo in pretiosam et vivificam crucem, et in secundum adventum, et de caritate et eleemosyna

Greek title: Λόγος εἰς τὸν τίμιον καὶ ζωοποιὸν σταυρὸν καὶ εἰς τὴν δευτέραν παρουσίαν. Καὶ περὶ ἀγάπης καὶ ἐλεημοσύνης

Work ID: Roger Pearse #54, TLG #53

K.G. Phrantzolas, Ὁσίου Ἐφραίμ τοῦ Σύρου ἔργα, vol. 4, Το Perivoli tis Panagias, 1992: 129-154.

20) On Patience and the Consummation of this Age ...
Latin title: De patientia et consummatione huius saeculi, ac de secundo aduentu; necnon de meditatione diuinarum scripturarum; et quae quantaque sit quietis silentiique utilitas.
Greek title: Περὶ ὑπομονῆς καὶ συντελείας καὶ τῆς δευτέρας παρουσίας. Καὶ περὶ μελέτης τῶν θείων Γραφῶν. Καὶ τί τὸ τῆς ἡσυχίας ὠφέλιμον.
Work ID: Roger Pearse #55, TLG #54
K.G. Phrantzolas, Ὁσίου Ἐφραίμ τοῦ Σύρου ἔργα, vol. 4, To Perivoli tis Panagias, 1992: 155-179.

21) On the Coming of the Lord (Sermons1-3)
Latin title: In adventum domini (sermo i-iii)
Greek title: Εἰς τὴν παρουσίαν τοῦ Κυρίου (I-III)
Work ID: Roger Pearse #56 for all, TLG #55, #56, #57
K.G. Phrantzolas, Ὁσίου Ἐφραίμ τοῦ Σύρου ἔργα, vol. 4, To Perivoli tis Panagias, 1992: 180-199.
much overlap with #53, many parts the same

22) Sermon on the Judgment and the Resurrection
Latin title: Sermo de iudicio et resurrectione
Greek title: Λόγος περὶ κρίσεως καὶ ἀναστάσεως
Work ID: Roger Pearse #57, TLG #58
K.G. Phrantzolas, Ὁσίου Ἐφραίμ τοῦ Σύρου ἔργα, vol. 4, To Perivoli tis Panagias, 1992: 200-205.

23) Exhortation on the Second Coming of the Lord and Repentance
Latin title: Sermo paraeneticus de secundo aduentu domini, et de paenitentia
Greek title: Λόγος παραινετικός. Περὶ τῆς δευτέρας παρουσίας τοῦ Κυρίου, καὶ περὶ μετανοίας
Work ID: Roger Pearse #58, TLG #59
K.G. Phrantzolas, Ὁσίου Ἐφραίμ τοῦ Σύρου ἔργα, vol. 4, To Perivoli tis Panagias, 1992: 206-222.

24) Sermon on the Second Coming and Judgment
Latin title: Sermo de secundo aduentu et iudicio
Greek title: Λόγος περὶ τῆς δευτέρας παρουσίας καὶ κρίσεως
Work ID: Roger Pearse #59, TLG #60
K.G. Phrantzolas, Ὁσίου Ἐφραίμ τοῦ Σύρου ἔργα, vol. 4, To Perivoli tis Panagias, 1992: 223-233.

25) Sermon on Repentance and Judgment
Latin title: Sermo de paenitentia et iudicio et separatione animae et corporis
Greek title: Λόγος περὶ μετανοίας καὶ κρίσεως, καὶ περὶ χωρισμοῦ ψυχῆς καὶ σώματος
Work ID: Roger Pearse #60, TLG #61
K.G. Phrantzolas, Ὁσίου Ἐφραίμ τοῦ Σύρου ἔργα, vol. 4, To Perivoli tis Panagias, 1992: 234-244.

26) Sermon on the Resurrection of the Dead
Latin title: De resurrectione mortuorum sermo
Greek title: Περὶ ἀναστάσεως νεκρῶν λόγος
Work ID: Roger Pearse #62, TLG #63
K.G. Phrantzolas, Ὁσίου Ἐφραίμ τοῦ Σύρου ἔργα, vol. 4, To Perivoli tis Panagias, 1992: 256-274.

27) Regarding Those Who Say There is No Resurrection
Latin title: De iis, qui dicunt resurrectionem mortuorum non esse
Greek title: Περί των λεγόντων μη είναι ανάστασιν
Work ID: Roger Pearse #63, TLG #64
K.G. Phrantzolas, Ὁσίου Ἐφραίμ τοῦ Σύρου ἔργα, vol. 4, To Perivoli tis Panagias, 1992: 275-289.

28) On the Phrase: Two Shall Be in the Field
Latin title: In illud: duo erunt in agro
Greek title: Τῷ δύο ἔσονται ἐν ἀγρῷ
Work ID: Roger Pearse #64, TLG #65
K.G. Phrantzolas, Ὁσίου Ἐφραίμ τοῦ Σύρου ἔργα, vol. 4, To Perivoli tis Panagias, 1992: 290-292.

29) On the Blessed Places
Latin title: De locis beatis
Greek title: Περί των μακαρίων τόπων
Work ID: Roger Pearse #67, TLG #68
K.G. Phrantzolas, Ὁσίου Ἐφραίμ τοῦ Σύρου ἔργα, vol. 4, To Perivoli tis Panagias, 1992: 298-302.

30) In This World You Shall Have Tribulation
Latin title (RP): In illud: In hoc mundo pressuram habebitis
Latin title (TLG): In sermonem, quem dixit dominus, quod: In hoc mundo pressuram habebitis, et de perfectione hominis
Greek title: Εἰς τὸν λόγον, ὃν εἶπεν ὁ Κύριος, ὅτι ἐν τῷ κόσμῳ τούτῳ θλῖψιν ἕξετε· καὶ περὶ τοῦ τέλειον εἶναι τὸν ἄνθρωπον
Work ID: Roger Pearse #72, TLG #73
K.G. Phrantzolas, Ὁσίου Ἐφραίμ τοῦ Σύρου ἔργα, vol. 4, To Perivoli tis Panagias, 1992: 333-398.

31) Concerning Those Who Entice You to Licentiousness
Latin title: De his, qui animas ad impudicitiam pelliciunt, cum dicant nihil mali esse
Greek title: Περί των δελεαζόντων ψυχάς προς ασέλγειαν, εν τω λέγειν, ότι ουδέν εστι το πράγμα
Work ID: Roger Pearse #91, TLG #92
K.G. Phrantzolas, Ὁσίου Ἐφραίμ τοῦ Σύρου ἔργα, vol. 5, To Perivoli tis Panagias, 1994: 207-223.

32) Exhortation on Silence and Quiet
Latin title: Adhortatio de silentio et quiete
Greek title: Παραίνεσις περί ησυχίας
Work ID: Roger Pearse #113, TLG #114
K.G. Phrantzolas, Ὁσίου Ἐφραίμ τοῦ Σύρου ἔργα, vol. 6, To Perivoli tis Panagias, 1995: 42-46.

33) Response to a Brother Concerning Eli the Priest
Latin title: Apologia ad fratrem quendam, de Heli sacerdote
Greek title: Ἀπολογία πρὸς ἀδελφὸν περὶ Ἠλὶ τοῦ ἱερέως
Work ID: Roger Pearse #119, TLG #120
K.G. Phrantzolas, Ὁσίου Ἐφραίμ τοῦ Σύρου ἔργα, vol. 6, To Perivoli tis Panagias, 1995: 81-90.

34) On Julian the Ascetic
Latin title: De Iuliano asceta
Greek title: Περί Ιουλιανού του ασκητού
Work ID: Roger Pearse, #122, TLG #123
K.G. Phrantzolas, Ὁσίου Ἐφραίμ τοῦ Σύρου ἔργα, vol. 6, To Perivoli tis Panagias, 1995: 119-130.

ENDNOTES

[1] This situation may be changing. According to blog post by Roger Pearse, a translation of the first of Phrantzolas' seven volumes of Ephraim's works, being published by St. Vladimir's Seminary Press, could be completed in 2024. See https://www.roger-pearse.com/weblog/2023/10/13/ephrem-graecus-published-english-translations-coming-soon/.
[2] See https://www.roger-pearse.com/.
[3] See https://www.roger-pearse.com/weblog/ephraim-graecus-works/.
[4] The TLG website is https://stephanus.tlg.uci.edu/index.php.
[5] This is the system used on TLG because it is the most convenient system available for the majority of his works.
[6] "The Saviour did this [sent the two witnesses] that he might demonstrate his inexplicable philanthropy. Because *not even in that season* does he allow mankind to be without preaching so that all might be without excuse in the judgment."
[7] "All who did not take the seal of the antichrist, and all who hid in the caves, shall rejoice with the bridegroom in the eternal, heavenly bridal chamber with all of the saints for unending ages of ages."
[8] The Greek here is ῥυσθῶμεν ἐκ θλίψεως τῆς μελλούσης ἔρχεσθαι ἐπὶ τῆς γῆς.
[9] The Greek here is διατηρεῖ αὐτούς.
[10] RP 49, TLG 48.406-407.
[11][11] For those who complained that I left out vital material in this selection, I here include the entire passage in Greek. Those who can read the Greek can easily ascertain that my ellipses did not affect the integrity of the passage whatsoever. Καὶ καθὼς ἐγένετο ἐν ταῖς ἡμέραις τοῦ Νῶε, κ. τ. λ. Οὕτω τοίνυν, ὡς εἴρηται, ἐκβληθέντος διὰ τὴν ἀποστασίαν τοῦ λόγου τοῦ εὐαγγελικοῦ, κατὰ τὴν ὁμοίωσιν τῶν ἐπὶ τοῦ κατακλυσμοῦ συμβεβηκότων, ὁ κατὰ τῶν ἀσεβῶν ὄλεθρος ἐπιστήσεται, φησί. Ἀλλ'

ὡς τότε πάντας μὲν ἀπώλεσεν, οὐ μὴν καὶ τοὺς συνηγμένους ἅμα τῷ Νῶε ἐν τῇ κιβωτῷ, οὕτω καὶ ἐπὶ τῆς αὐτοῦ παρουσίας οἱ μὲν ἀσεβεῖς κατὰ τὸν καιρὸν τῆς ἀποστασίας τρυφαῖς καὶ μέθαις καὶ γάμοις καὶ ταῖς τοῦ βίου ἡδοναῖς κατατριβόμενοι ὁμοίως τοῖς ἐπὶ τοῦ Νῶε κατακλυσθέντες ἀπολοῦνται. Ὑπὲρ δὲ τοῦ μή τινα νομίσαι δι' ὕδατος καὶ τούτους κατακλυσθήσεσθαι, ἀναγκαίως τῷ ἐπὶ τοῦ Λὼτ κέχρηται παραδείγματι, Καθὼς ἐγένετο, λέγων, ἐν ταῖς ἡμέραις Λώτ, ἤσθιον, ἔπινον, καὶ τὰ ἑξῆς· Ἡ δὲ ἡμέρα ἐξῆλθε Λὼτ ἀπὸ Σοδόμων ἔβρεξε πῦρ ἀπ' οὐρανοῦ καὶ ἀπώλεσε πάντας. Κατὰ τὰ αὐτὰ ἔσται ᾗ ἡμέρᾳ ὁ Υἱὸς τοῦ ἀνθρώπου ἀποκαλύπτεται· σφόδρα ἀπορρήτως καὶ φοβερῶς διδάσκων ὅτι πυρὶ καὶ θείῳ ἀπ' οὐρανοῦ καταπεμπομένῳ τοὺς ἀσεβεῖς πάντας ἡ ὀργὴ μετελεύσεται· διὸ τοῖς μὲν ἡμέραν ταύτην ἐπιστῆναι εὐχομένοις ἀσεβέσιν ἡ προφητικὴ φωνὴ ἐπανατείνεται λέγουσα· Οὐαὶ οἱ ἐπιθυμοῦντες τὴν ἡμέραν Κυρίου! Ἵνα τί; Ὑμῖν αὕτη ἔσται σκότος, καὶ οὐ φῶς, ἡμέρα σκότους καὶ γνόφου, ἡμέρα ταλαιπωρίας καὶ ἀφανισμοῦ. Σφόδρα δὲ ἀκριβῶς καὶ ἐνταῦθα ἐτήρησεν ὁ Σωτὴρ οὐ πρότερον τὸ πῦρ εἰπὼν ἀπ' οὐρανοῦ καὶ τὸ θεῖον κατεληλυθέναι ἐπὶ τοὺς ἐν Σοδόμοις ἀσεβεῖς, ἢ τὸν Λὼτ ἐξελθεῖν, καὶ χωρισθῆναι ἐξ αὐτῶν. Οὕτω καὶ ἐπὶ τοῦ κατακλυσμοῦ οὐ πρότερον ἐπῆλθεν οὗτος καὶ πάντας ἀπώλεσε τοὺς κατὰ γῆν οἰκοῦντας, ἢ τὸν Νῶε εἰσελθεῖν εἰς τὴν κιβωτόν. Κατὰ τὰ αὐτὰ τοίνυν καὶ ἐπὶ τῆς συντελείας οὐ πρότερον ἔσεσθαι τὸν κατακλυσμὸν τῆς ἀπωλείας τῶν ἀσεβῶν φησιν, ἢ συναχθῆναι εἰς τὴν ἐπουράνιον τοῦ Θεοῦ κιβωτὸν, καὶ διασωθῆναι τοὺς τότε εὑρεθησομένους τοῦ Θεοῦ ἀνθρώπους, κατὰ τὸ παράδειγμα τὸ ἐπὶ τοῦ Νῶε· οἷς καὶ λεχθήσεται κατὰ καιρὸν τὸ προφητικὸν ἐκεῖνο· «Βάδιζε, λαός μου, εἴσελθε εἰς τὸ ταμεῖόν σου, καὶ τὰ ἑξῆς, ἕως οὗ παρέλθοι ἡ ὀργὴ Κυρίου»· ὥσπερ καὶ ἐπὶ τοῦ Λὼτ ἐποίησεν, ἵνα μὴ οἱ δίκαιοι συναπόλωνται τοῖς ἀσεβέσιν· οὕτως καὶ ἐπὶ τῆς συντελείας τοῦ αἰῶνος οὐ πρότερον αὕτη ἔσται, ἢ πάντας τοὺς ἐπὶ γῆς δικαίους καὶ θεοσεβεῖς ἀφορισθῆναι τῶν ἀσεβῶν, καὶ συναχθῆναι εἰς τὴν ἐπουράνιον τοῦ Θεοῦ κιβωτόν· οὕτω γὰρ μηκέτι μηδενὸς δικαίου ἐν ἀνθρώποις εὑρισκομένου, πάντων δὲ ἀθέων ἀσεβῶν τῶν ὑπὸ τοῦ Ἀντιχρίστου γεγονότων, τῆς τε ἀποστασίας καθ' ὅλης τῆς οἰκουμένης κρατησάσης, ἡ τοῦ Θεοῦ ὀργὴ τοὺς ἀσεβεῖς μετελεύσεται.

[12] The cited passage is Jeremiah 23:7-8. The brackets in this citation present an obvious ellipsis due to homoioteleuton (having the same ending), not from the original author but a later copyist. Irenaeus makes

a similar observation in *Against Heresies 5.32.2* where he states, "For his seed is the church, which receives the adoption to God through the Lord." The main focus of the 32nd chapter is defending the truth that all the seed of Abraham (Jacob and the Gentiles of this age) shall receive their inheritance in the resurrection.

[13] The order in Harvey's Latin and Greek edition varies in places in the 4th chapter. In Harvey's edition, the correct address is 4.48.1-2.

[14] The Latin reads, duae synagogae, id est duae congregationes. Both terms are used in the general sense of assemblies or gatherings of believers.

[15] The cited passage is Jeremiah 23:7-8. The brackets in this citation present an obvious ellipsis due to homoioteleuton (having the same ending), not from the original author but a later copyist.

[16] God returning to the Jewish temple and owning it as his temple is absolutely critical for the antichrist scenario to play out. If the Jews built a physical temple today in the church age (when the church is the temple of God), and an ungodly man sat in the Jewish temple and declared himself god, that act would be sacrilegious, but it would not be the abomination of desolation. The antichrist's actions are an abomination precisely because the temple is the temple of God. God owns it as his temple on earth. His name and His honor are there, the same way it was until the day that the vail was rent and the temple was disowned.

[17] The cited passage is Revelation 13:5-10.

[18] Irenaeus' portrayal of the tribulation saints presents precisely what we see in the Bible. Every passage in sacred writ which presents saints in the tribulation portrays them as practicing Jewish believers not as practicing Christians. For instance, Matthew 24 presents believers who worship at a temple owned by God and are obligated by God to keep the sabbath. Revelation 11 presents God as owning the temple and those who worship in its precincts. It also presents the two witnesses calling down fire and plagues from heaven, something entirely contrary to the church age. But such religion and such vengeance perfectly harmonize with a seventieth week that is the same Jewish dispensation as the first sixty-nine weeks.

[19] Irenaeus starts out *Against Heresies, 5.35.1* with the line, "If, however, any shall endeavour to allegorize [prophecies] of this kind, they shall not be found consistent with themselves in all points, and shall be confuted by the teaching of the very expressions [in question]." The Latin introduction to the chapter summarizes thusly, "He contends that these testimonies already alleged cannot be understood allegorically of celestial blessings, but that they shall have their fulfillment after the coming of antichrist, and the resurrection, in the terrestrial Jerusalem. To the former prophecies he subjoins others drawn from Isaiah, Jeremiah, and the Apocalypse of John."

[20] See, for instance, William Watson, *Dispensationalism Before Darby*, Lampion, 2015. He presents many examples of men and women, clergy and laymen, who held a pretribulation rapture prior to Darby.

[21] See, for instance, the points I make in the relevant appendices in *The Demonic Delusion of Robert Baxter*. Robert was a prophet in the Irvingite movement for a while, the same group with which Margaret McDonald was associated. The rapture teaching of this group was distinctly prewrath, with the church going through 3.5 years of tribulation before being raptured prior to a short time of judgment that would fall upon the world before the second coming proper. The group received this rapture teaching from Margaret McDonald, who received it by a revelation supposedly from the Holy Spirit. She clearly articulates this prewrath view of the rapture in her own written testimony on the revelation that she had been given.

[22] *The Collected Writings of J.N. Darby*, Vol. 11, p. 67.

Made in the USA
Middletown, DE
03 July 2025